THE HERSCHEL HOBBS COMMENTARY

STUDYING ADULT LIFE AND WORK LESSONS

by

HERSCHEL H. HOBBS

ROSS H. McLAREN

&

ROBERT J. DEAN

SUMMER 1998

Volume 30, Number 4

ROSS H. McLAREN
Biblical Studies Specialist

Carolyn Gregory
Production Specialist

Stephen Smith
Graphic Designer

Carla Dickerson
Technical Specialist

Send questions/comments to
Ross H. McLaren, editor
127 9th Ave., North
Nashville, TN 37234-0175
Email: HHobbsComm@bssb.com

Management Personnel

Rick Edwards, *Manager*
Adult Biblical Studies Section
Louis B. Hanks, *Director,*
Biblical Studies Department
Ken Marler, *Team Leader*
Age Group Field Services Team
_____ , *Team Leader*
Age Group Ministry Design and
Resources Team

BILL L. TAYLOR, *Director*
Bible Teaching-Reaching Division

ACKNOWLEDGMENTS.–We believe the Bible has God for its author, salvation for its end, and truth, without any mixture of error, for its matter. The 1963 statement of *The Baptist Faith and Message* is our doctrinal guideline.

Unless otherwise indicated, all Scripture quotations are from the *King James Version.* This translation is available in a Holman Bible and can be ordered through Baptist Book Stores or Lifeway Christian Stores.

Quotations marked Beck are from *The Holy Bible: An American Translation* by William F. Beck. Copyright © Mrs. William F. Beck, 1976. Published by Leader Publishing Company. Used by permission. Scripture quotations identified as CEV are from the *Contemporary English Version.* Copyright © American Bible Society 1991, 1992. Used by permission. Excerpts from *The Jerusalem Bible,* copyright © 1966 by Darton, Longman and Todd, Ltd., and Doubleday and Company, Inc. Used by permission of the publisher. Verses marked TLB are taken from *The Living Bible.* Copyright © Tyndale House Publishers, Wheaton, Illinois, 1971. Used by permission. Passages marked NASB are from the *New American Standard Bible: 1995 Update.* © The Lockman Foundation, 1960, 1962, 1963, 1968, 1971, 1972, 1973, 1975, 1977, 1995. Used by permission. This translation is available in a Holman Bible and can be ordered through Baptist Book Stores or Lifeway Christian Stores. Quotations marked NCV are from The Holy Bible, *New Century Version.* Copyright © 1987, 1988, 1991 by Word Publishing, Dallas, Texas 75039. Used by permission. Quotations marked NEB are from *The New English Bible.* Copyright © The Delegates of the Oxford University Press and the Syndics of the Cambridge University Press, 1961, 1970. Reprinted by permission. Quotations marked NIV are from the Holy Bible, *New International Version,* copyright © 1973, 1978, 1984 by International Bible Society. This translation is available in a Holman Bible and can be ordered through Baptist Book Stores or Lifeway Christian Stores. Excerpts from *The New Jerusalem Bible,* copyright © 1985 by Darton, Longman and Todd, Ltd., and Doubleday and Company, Inc. Used by permission of the publisher. Scripture quotations marked NLT are taken from the *Holy Bible, New Living Translation,* copyright © 1996. Used by permission of Tyndale House Publishers, Inc., Wheaton, Illinois 60189. All rights reserved. Quotations marked NRSV are from the *New Revised Standard Version of the Bible,* copyright © 1989 by the Division of Christian Education

(Continued on page iv)

CONTENTS

Dedicated to

Ken Sande,

a Christian attorney and
executive director of Peacemaker Ministries,
who freely gave us his time, shared with us his ideas and
materials, and personally embodies the principles of peacemaking
he seeks to impart to and cultivate among the Lord's people.

Matthew 5:9

(Acknowledgments continued from page ii)

of the National Council of the Churches of Christ in the United States of America. Used by permission. All rights reserved. Quotations marked Phillips are reprinted with permission of Macmillan Publishing Co., Inc. from J. B. Phillips: *The New Testament In Modern English*, Revised Edition. © J. B. Phillips 1958, 1960, 1972. Quotations marked REB are from *The Revised English Bible*. Copyright © Oxford University Press and Cambridge University Press, 1989. Reprinted by permission. Quotations marked RSV are from the *Revised Standard Version of the Bible*, copyright 1946, 1952, © 1971, 1973 by the Division of Christian Education of the National Council of Churches of Christ in the U.S.A., and used by permission. Quotations marked GNB or TEV are from the *Good News Bible*, the Bible in Today's Modern English Version. Old Testament: Copyright © American Bible Society 1976; New Testament: Copyright © American Bible Society 1966, 1971, 1976. Used by permission. Quotations marked TCNT are from *The Twentieth Century New Testament*, copyright © 1904 Fleming H. Revell Co. Quotations marked Williams are from *Williams New Testament in the Language of the People*, by Charles B. Williams. Copyright © 1937, 1966, 1986 by Holman Bible Publishers.

The Herschel Hobbs Commentary (ISSN 0191-4219), *Studying Adult Life and Work Lessons*, is published quarterly for adult teachers and members using the Life and Work Series by the Sunday School Board of the Southern Baptist Convention, 127 Ninth Avenue, North, Nashville, Tennessee 37234: James T. Draper, Jr., President; O. Eugene Mims, Vice-President, Church Growth Group; Bill L. Taylor, Director, Bible Teaching-Reaching Division. Printed in the U.S. Single subscription to individual address, $20.50 per year. If you need help with an order, WRITE Customer Service Center, 127 Ninth Avenue, North, Nashville, TN 37234-0113; FAX (615) 251-5933; or EMAIL to CompuServe ID 70423,2526. Mail address changes to *The Herschel Hobbs Commentary, Studying Adult Life and Work Lessons*, Customer Service Center, 127 Ninth Avenue, North, Nashville, TN 37234-0113. © Copyright 1998 The Sunday School Board of the Southern Baptist Convention. All rights reserved.

STUDY THEME: OVERCOMING HINDRANCES TO SPIRITUAL GROWTH

June 7

UNRESOLVED ANGER

Background Scripture: Genesis 4:1-16;
             Ephesians 4:26-27,31; James 1:19-20
Focal Verses: Genesis 4:2b-8; Ephesians 4:26-27,31;
             James 1:19-20

INTRODUCTION

1. Many Christians today, including those in Southern Baptist churches, show little evidence that they are experiencing significant spiritual growth.

2. One of the reasons for this lack of spiritual growth is that many Christians have fallen prey to things that hinder their spiritual growth. Four of these hindrances to spiritual growth are unresolved anger, an unforgiving spirit, apathy, and self-centeredness.

3. This week's lesson begins a new study theme on "Overcoming Hindrances to Spiritual Growth." The four lessons of this study theme focus on believers' recognizing and overcoming these specific hindrances to their spiritual growth.

4. The first lesson focuses on unresolved anger. The Lesson Bible Truth is that unresolved anger prevents a believer from becoming what God wants the person to be.

5. Thus the question this lesson addresses is, How can I deal with my anger?

6. The Lesson Outcome is to help you realize the destructive nature of unresolved anger, be motivated to deal with anger in constructive ways, and identify steps you will take to resolve anger caused by one specific thing.

I. SOME PRELIMINARY CONSIDERATIONS

1. The Contemporary Context

Many adults are allowing unresolved anger to diminish their lives and their effectiveness as Christians. For some, anger is their favorite feeling; they like feeling angry and constantly find something or someone on which to focus their anger. Others have free-floating anger that is an accumulation from various sources and that may be directed at unsuspecting, innocent people. Still others are angry and do not like the feeling. They hate that they are angry and want to get rid of their anger. Angry adults need to be aware of the destructive effects of anger on them and on people who bear the brunt of their anger. These adults need to recognize the reality and the intensity of their anger, identify anger's source, and move to deal with their anger in constructive ways. This lesson is an attempt to help them do so.

2. Anger

An angry man—there is my story: the bitter rancor of Achilles, prince of the house of Peleus, which brought a thousand troubles upon the Achaian host. Many a strong soul it sent down to Hades, and left the heroes themselves a prey to dogs and carrion birds, while the will of God moved on to fulfillment.

Any high school student would recognize these opening words from Book I of one of the oldest and most read stories in literature—*The Iliad*—Homer's story of one angry man, Achilles.

Make no mistake about it, anger is a fact of life. *Everyone experiences anger.* True, there is a valid, positive type of anger, such as Jesus demonstrated when He cleansed the temple. But this "righteous anger" is not the subject of this lesson. This lesson focuses on destructive anger. Of this destructive type of anger Gary Jackson Oliver and H. Norman Wright (*When*

Anger Hits Home [Chicago: Moody Press, 1992], 12) wrote,
"Anger motivates a person to hate, wound, damage, annihilate,
despise, scorn, loathe, vilify, curse, ruin, and demolish. Under
anger's curse a [person] will ridicule, get even with, laugh at,
humiliate, shame, criticize, bawl out, fight, crush, offend, or
bully another person."

> Anger in its time and place
> May assume a kind of grace.
> It must have some reason in it,
> And not last beyond a minute.
> If to further lengths it go,
> It does into malice grow.
> 'Tis the difference that we see
> 'Twixt the serpent and the bee.
> If the latter you provoke,
> It inflicts a hasty stroke,
> Puts you to some little pain,
> But it *never stings again.*
> Close in tufted bush or brake
> Lurks the poison-swelled snake
> Nursing up his cherished wrath;
> In the purlieus of his path,
> In the cold, or in the warm,
> Mean him good, or mean him harm,
> Wheresoever fate may bring you,
> The vile snake will *always sting you.*

("Anger," by Charles and Mary Lamb. *The Book of Virtues,* ed.
by William J. Bennett [New York: Simon & Schuster, 1993], 40.)

Oliver and Wright also addressed unresolved anger. They
wrote, "Ignoring anger is an unhealthy choice. In the short-term
it hinders us from dealing with the real issues, and in the long-
term it significantly increases the probability of physical problems." They concluded, "Ignoring your experiences of anger is
usually hazardous to your emotional, psychological, physical,
and spiritual health" (*When Anger Hits Home,* 54-55). Hence the
importance of this lesson.

II. FOCAL VERSES EXAMINED
(Gen. 4:2b-8; Eph. 4:26-27,31; Jas. 1:19-20)

Genesis 4 tells the story of Cain and Abel and their freewill offerings to the Lord. When God responded favorably to Abel's offering but rejected Cain's offering, Cain became extremely angry and murdered his brother. James, the brother of our Lord, told his readers that anger does not produce the righteous life God wants for His people. Paul warned the Ephesian believers not to sin by harboring unresolved anger. They were to resolve their anger quickly, lest they should give the devil an opportunity to do his work.

1. Causes of Anger (Gen. 4:2b-5)

In due time following the expulsion from Eden, Adam "knew" Eve. In the Old Testament this verb is used in a conjugal sense. As a result, Eve conceived and gave birth to Cain, their first-born. A second son was named Abel.

Verses 2b-5: **And Abel was a keeper of sheep, but Cain was a tiller of the ground. ³And in the process of time it came to pass, that Cain brought of the fruit of the ground an offering unto the LORD. ⁴And Abel, he also brought of the firstlings of his flock and of the fat thereof. And the LORD had respect unto Abel and to his offering: ⁵but unto Cain and to his offering he had not respect. And Cain was very wroth, and his countenance fell.**

Cain became a farmer; Abel became a shepherd. Nothing is said about the Lord commanding that an offering be brought to Him. The account also is silent about a stated altar or if a certain type of offering was to be made. Evidently both brothers were religious, and each brought the product of his labor as an offering to God.

Yet **the Lord had respect unto Abel and to his offering.** That is, "the Lord looked with favor on Abel and his offering," but not on Cain and his offering. Why? Various suggestions have been made. One suggestion is that God did not approve of produce or agricultural offerings but did desire blood offerings. Leviticus 2:1, however, does allow offerings other than flesh and blood, specifically grain offerings (the KJV uses the word "meat" to describe this offering—which today is confusing since the word *meat* in 1611 meant "meal"). True, animal sacrifices were required for a sin offering, but that does not seem to be the case here. Another suggestion is that Cain's offering was not acceptable because it was from the cursed ground (3:17). Still another suggestion is that Cain's offering reflected the work of his own hands, what he grew, but Abel's offering involved life, which only God can give. But as is the case with animal life so it is with agricultural life—only God can cause produce to grow. One other suggestion is that God was displeased with the proportion of Cain's offering, but the Scripture does not support this idea.

Nothing is said about how God indicated His acceptance of Abel and his offering and His rejection of Cain and his offering. Hebrews 11:3 says, "By faith Abel offered unto God a more excellent sacrifice than Cain, by which he obtained witness that he was righteous, God testifying of his gifts." This gives us a clue. The difference may lie in the attitude of each brother.

Notice that Abel brought of the **firstlings of his flock.** Nothing is said about Cain bringing the firstfruits of his harvest. The omission may be significant. If so, this implies that Abel brought the best of his lambs, while Cain simply brought something— not of poor quality, but not his *best* or the firstfruits.

Clyde T. Francisco ("Genesis," *The Broadman Bible Commentary*, vol. 1, rev. ed. [Nashville: Broadman Press, 1973], 133) commented, "Cain was grateful to God for a successful year of farming; he wanted to thank him for his help; so he brought him a present. Abel in giving God his best . . . witnessed to his total dependence upon God, his indebtedness to him. Cain thanked God for serving him. Abel confessed himself to be a servant of God."

Thus we see the difference in attitude on the part of the two brothers. Cain made God a gift in recognition of God's help. Abel first gave himself to God, his offering being the evidence of it.

Cain's reaction revealed his overall attitude. Cain became **very wroth, and his countenance fell. Cain was very**

wroth literally reads, "it became hot to him." His **countenance** refers to his "face." Here is both *anger* and *dejection.*

Resentment, jealousy, and rejection evidently generated Cain's anger. Our anger can have numerous other sources. In fact, rarely is there only one cause of our anger. Usually several factors contribute to it. "Many factors influence, contribute to, and maintain anger" (Oliver and Wright, *When Anger Hits Home,* 92). Oliver and Wright further noted that any number of situations can *trigger* an anger response, but they pointed to 10 major factors that *contribute* to the arousal of anger in most people: childhood experiences, physiological factors, accumulated stress from normal everyday events, injustice, low self-esteem, worry, conflict, fear, hurt, and frustration—the number one cause (*When Anger Hits Home,* 91-107).

As believers, we need to identify the causes of our anger so that we can take steps to resolve it. Unless and until we are willing to deal with the issues, factors, and causes underlying our anger, we will not be able to resolve it.

2. Caution Against Anger (Gen. 4:6-8)

In such a state the Lord confronted Cain.

Verses 6-7: **And the LORD said unto Cain, Why art thou wroth? and why is thy countenance fallen? ⁷If thou doest well, shalt thou not be accepted? and if thou doest not well, sin lieth at the door. And unto thee shall be his desire, and thou shalt rule over him.**

Anger and a sense of dejection are natural responses to rejection, but they should not lead to sin. God challenged Cain to control his emotions rather than to be mastered by them. When emotions are like wild horses, there is a danger that they may get out of control, run away, wreck the buggy, and kill the driver. Such power under control, however, can be useful to the driver.

The Lord reminded Cain that he could profit by his experience, if he willed to do so. If he brought his next offering in faith, he and his offering would be accepted. If he let his anger control him, the result would be further disaster.

The Lord warned Cain that **sin lieth at the door.** The Lord likened sin to a wild animal crouching at Cain's door, ready to pounce on him the moment he opened the door. Its desire was to destroy Cain. Instead, Cain needed to "master" (NIV) or **rule over** it.

Cain, however, allowed his anger to seethe in his breast. Rather than control his "wild horses," he let them hurtle him to disaster.

Verse 8: **And Cain talked with Abel his brother: and it came to pass, when they were in the field, that Cain rose up against Abel his brother, and slew him.**

Though the Lord knew what was in Cain's heart, apparently Abel was unaware of it. Some ancient versions of this passage add "Let's go out to the field" after the first phrase (see the NIV). This additional phrase that does not appear in the Hebrew Masoretic text does not affect the meaning of the story, although it does serve to indicate Cain's premeditated intention. Cain's act was cold, premeditated murder! **In the field** was probably an out-of-the-way place where Cain thought no one else would see what transpired. Suddenly and without warning, Cain **rose up** and **slew** his unsuspecting **brother.**

The story of Cain and Abel reminds us that as Christians we need to be aware of the severe dangers that nurtured and unresolved anger pose. Too often we harbor anger. Too often we allow anger to be unresolved within us. Unresolved anger is dangerous. Unresolved anger affects the person who is angry. Unresolved anger can harm a person's relationship to God and hinder spiritual growth. Unresolved anger affects other people. Unresolved anger may escalate to further sinful action or violence.

3. Consequence of Anger (Jas. 1:19-20)

In James's exhortation, which he addressed to his **beloved brethren,** he wrote about the negative consequence of anger.

Verses 19-20: **Wherefore, my beloved brethren, let every man be swift to hear, slow to speak, slow to wrath: [20]for the wrath of man worketh not the righteousness of God.**

Let . . . be (*esto*) is an imperative, so a command. It also carries a note of urgency. This urgent imperative is inclusive. It involves **every man** or "everyone" (NIV). This urgent imperative includes three elements: **swift to hear, slow to speak, slow to wrath.**

Swift to hear means to be attentive. "The Greek moralists often urge a quick and attentive ear" (A. T. Robertson, *Word Pictures in the New Testament,* vol. 6 [Nashville: Broadman Press, 1933], 21). This admonition could include listening to a preacher's sermon or a teacher's lesson. Failure at this point will block the acceptance of the truth.

A little boy was restless and constantly squirming during the church service. The father told his wife he was going to have a session with him when they got home. On the way home the mother asked the boy what he got out of the pastor's sermon. He began to tell the many things he remembered. Arriving home the session was not forthcoming. Finally, the mother asked her husband why he had not talked to the son. The husband grinned and said, "He got more out of the sermon than I did."

Slow to speak means "slow to begin speaking" not "slow while speaking." The exhortation suggests restrained speech. A constant talker will not hear what another person says or even what God says. Too often we reverse this exhortation in practice. We are slow to hear and swift to speak!

Slow to wrath is connected to slow to speak as swift to speak would be connected to swift to wrath. In other words, rashness of speech is connected to anger or wrath. The word for **wrath** (*orge*) is not a sudden outburst of anger (*thumos*). *Orge* means an abiding, deep-seated anger. Such a wrath deters understanding and warps the spirit. James said that this wrath **worketh not the righteousness of God** in us or "does not bring about the righteous life that God desires" (NIV). **Not** is the strong negative *ouk*.

Orge most certainly does not produce righteousness—and that's the consequence of anger! Anger prevents Christians from developing a lifestyle that reflects God's character. Because anger prevents Christians from developing a lifestyle that reflects God's character, we are to resist becoming angry.

4. Constructive Approach to Resolving Anger (Eph. 4:26-27,31)

There is a better way to deal with our anger—get rid of it!
Verses 26-27: Be ye angry, and sin not: let not the sun go down upon your wrath: ²⁷neither give place to the devil.

Be ye angry, and sin not is actually a quotation from Psalm 4:4 in the Septuagint, the Greek translation of the Old Testament.

Be angry renders the Greek word *orgizesthe.* The noun form (*orge,* "wrath") means an abiding anger. When this word is used of God, it denotes His abiding, universal opposition to evil. When this word is applied to human beings, it expresses not a temper tantrum but deep-seated, abiding anger. Here the verb is an imperative form. A. T. Robertson (*Word Pictures in the New Testament,* vol. 4 [Nashville: Broadman Press, 1931], 540) called it a "permissive imperative." In other words, Paul did not command believers to be angry, but he acknowledged a concession: "You may be angry."

In the sense of God's opposition to evil, there are some things about which Christians should be angry: injustice, immorality, the narcotic traffic, economic oppression, and political corruption. Paul, however, was thinking about person-to-person relationships. He recognized that situations arise in which Christians do become angry. In such cases, one must express the anger in a responsible way. As Curtis Vaughan reminded us, "Anger that is selfish, undisciplined, and uncontrolled is always sinful; and even that which starts out as righteous indignation all too easily degenerates to this level" (*Ephesians: A Study Guide Commentary* [Grand Rapids: Zondervan Publishing House, 1977], 103).

Thus Paul strongly qualified the permission "If you are angry" (NEB, REB) with two additional statements. First, anger must be guarded carefully so it does not become sinful (v. 26a). Second, anger must never be harbored in our hearts (v. 26b). **Let not the sun go down upon your wrath** means that anger is not to be held on to until the next day. Though real, anger should be temporary. If it occurs, it must be held only briefly and then expelled without being allowed to smolder overnight. The important point is that anger that is not disposed of speedily soon takes deep root in one's heart. The word for **wrath** in verse 26 (*parorgismos*) is used only here in the New Testament, though it was used in the Septuagint. It refers specifically to anger that has been provoked.

When we store up anger in our hearts, we **give place to the devil** (*diabolos,* the "slanderer"). But we must not give the devil an opportunity in our lives. The Greek word *topon* means "foothold" (NIV). The devil must not be permitted to use our lives as a base of operations to perpetrate all kinds of evil. We must ever be on guard against him. Unresolved anger gives the devil room to act, a foothold from which he can exploit us.

Verse 31: **Let all bitterness, and wrath, and anger, and clamor, and evil speaking, be put away from you, with all malice.**

Paul then listed six specific aspects of anger that believers are to remove from their lives. **Bitterness** (*pikria*) denotes the sour, resentful spirit of one who harbors or stores up the injuries and insults from others, refusing to forgive or to be reconciled. **Bitterness,** or the hard-heartedness that harbors resentment about the past, will eat away at you if you do not "get rid of" it (NIV). In verse 31 the word **wrath** ("rage," NIV) translates *thumos,* which describes the furious burning of dry grass; it burns rapidly and then is over. *Thumos* is a sudden outburst of fury, the initial explosion of rage, that is of short duration. With this type of anger, when it's hot, it's very hot! (We get our English words *thermometer, thermostat,* and *thermos* from this Greek word.) **Anger** renders *orge,* the deep-seated, abiding kind of wrath, the settled hostility toward another. **Clamor** (*krauge*) or "brawling" (NIV) literally refers to "shouting." It indicates the lack of restraint that erupts in angry yelling. **Evil speaking** or "slander" (NIV), literally "blasphemy" (*blasphemia*), here indicates the angry abuse and vilifying of others that angry people pour forth. Perhaps **clamor** denotes public quarreling and **evil speaking** denotes slanderous whispers (Vaughan, *Ephesians,* 104). **Malice** (*kakia*) is a generalizing term that refers to spite or to a vicious disposition. It refers to wickedness and that which is evil.

As Andrew T. Lincoln pointed out ("Ephesians," in the *Word Biblical Commentary* [Dallas: Word Books, 1990], 309), within this "comprehensive listing there is also a progression from anger's inner center (*pikria*; 'bitterness') through it initial eruption (*thumos*; 'wrath' or 'rage') and steady festering (*orge*; 'anger') to its external expression (*krauge*; 'clamor' or 'brawling') and damaging of others (*blasphemia*; 'evil speaking' or 'slander')."

Anger is a major characteristic and disposition of the old pre-Christian life that is to be discarded. All of these vices related to anger are to be **put away from you** as one would "get rid of" (NIV) old garments.

Edwin Stanton, Secretary of War under Abraham Lincoln, was well-known for having an explosive temper. On one occasion during the darkest days of the Civil War, Stanton went to see Lincoln about the actions of a certain general. Lincoln let Stanton vent his anger. When Stanton finally exclaimed, "I'd like to write him a letter and tell him what I think of him!" Lincoln responded, "Well, why not do it? Sit down and write him a letter, saying all you have said to me." Stanton, surprised that Lincoln did not object to this course of action, promptly wrote the general a scathing letter telling him just what he thought of him. A couple of days later Stanton showed the letter to Lincoln, who acknowledged that Stanton certainly had raked the general over the coals and torn him to shreds. Then Lincoln asked, "Now, what are you going to do with this letter?" "Mail it," replied Stanton. "I wouldn't," replied the president quietly. Then Lincoln invited Stanton to throw the letter into the fireplace.

And that's what we all need to do with our unresolved anger—consign it to the flames! Remember, *anger* is just one letter short of *danger.*

June 14

AN UNFORGIVING SPIRIT

Background Scripture: Luke 15:25-30; 17:3-4;
Ephesians 4:32–5:2
Focal Verses: Luke 15:25-30; 17:3-4; Ephesians 4:32–5:2

INTRODUCTION

1. This week's lesson focuses on another hindrance to spiritual growth—an unforgiving spirit. This hindrance is closely related to the hindrance we examined last week—unresolved anger. An unforgiving spirit will grow out of unresolved anger, and unresolved anger will grow into an unforgiving spirit. It's a deadly two-way street.

2. Sometimes it's difficult, very difficult, to forgive someone who has wronged you—especially if that person is or was dear to you. But what's even more difficult is to live with the result of cultivating an unforgiving spirit—for such will not only hinder your spiritual growth, but it will change you for the worse. It will turn you into a bitter person.

3. Thus every believer should ask himself or herself, Why should I forgive people who have wronged me?

4. The Lesson Bible Truth is that Christians are to have a forgiving spirit because through Christ, God has forgiven them.

5. The Lesson Outcome is to help you understand reasons you are to be forgiving, be moved to forgive people who have wronged you, and extend forgiveness to specific people.

I. SOME PRELIMINARY CONSIDERATIONS

1. The Contemporary Context

For most adults, forgiving people who have offended them once is hard; to forgive a second time is often out of the question. Such adults rationalize their failure to forgive and hold on to malignant bitterness. But adults who refuse to forgive really block God's forgiveness from their lives. They nurture grudges. Such cultivated grudges adversely affect physical health and stymie spiritual growth. Unforgiving adults need to experience the freedom that comes from letting go of real or imagined offenses against them. They need to find their model and motivation for forgiving in God's forgiveness extended to them in Christ. They need to shed the self-imposed weight of an unforgiving spirit that impedes their spiritual progress.

2. An Unforgiving Spirit

Charles R. Swindoll rightly has said, "There is no torment like the inner torment of an unforgiving spirit. It refuses to be soothed, it refuses to be healed, it refuses to forget" (quoted in Edythe Draper, *Draper's Book of Quotations for the Christian World* [Wheaton: Tyndale House Publishers, Inc., 1992], 531).

II. FOCAL VERSES EXAMINED
(Luke 15:25-30; 17:3-4; Eph. 4:32–5:2)

In the actions and words of the prodigal's older brother in Luke 15, we may view a portrait of a person with an unforgiving spirit. In Luke 17 Jesus commanded His followers to have a forgiving spirit—a willingness to forgive repeatedly someone who does them wrong. In Ephesians 4 Paul taught believers that the way to overcome an unforgiving spirit is through love, God's *agape* love in us.

1. Portrait of an Unforgiving Spirit (Luke 15:25-30)

Luke 15 contains three parables showing rejoicing over the *lost* being found. Our lesson involves the third of the parables in this chapter, the return of the prodigal son. Not everyone was joyful over the younger son's return. The older son evidenced anger, bitterness, and an unforgiving spirit toward both his younger brother and toward his father.

Verses 25-28: **Now his elder son was in the field: and as he came and drew nigh to the house, he heard music and dancing. ²⁶And he called one of the servants, and asked what these things meant. ²⁷And he said unto him, Thy brother is come; and thy father hath killed the fatted calf, because he hath received him safe and sound. ²⁸And he was angry, and would not go in: therefore came his father out, and entreated him.**

Perhaps such happy occasions had been rare, if not nonexistent, since the younger son left home. On hearing the cause of the celebration, the older son became **angry.** A. T. Robertson (*Word Pictures in the New Testament,* vol. 2 [Nashville: Broadman Press, 1930], 212) called this an ingressive passive aorist form. *Ingressive* means that the action is regarded from the viewpoint of its initiation. The passive voice means that this news made him angry. Thus the aorist tense may read "he flew into a rage" or "he became enraged." Although his father's perceived lenient favoritism was the immediate cause of the older son's anger, the older brother must have had other causes that laid behind his unforgiving spirit since the word is *orgisthe,* from *orge,* referring to a deep-seated, abiding anger. This deep-seated anger probably had been in the older son's heart for a long while. He had developed an unforgiving spirit. The news of the younger brother's return drew it into overt action.

When the father heard about his older son's response, he went out to plead with his son to join the festivities.

Verses 29-30: **And he answering said to his father, Lo, these many years do I serve thee, neither transgressed I at anytime thy commandment: and yet thou never gavest me a kid, that I might make merry with my friends: ³⁰but as soon as this thy son was come, which hath devoured thy living with harlots, thou hast killed for him the fatted calf.**

The elder son never referred to the younger son as his brother but as **thy son.** Unlike the younger son, the older one never had left his father geographically. But in his spirit he had been in a much farther country than the younger son. The younger son returned to his father; the older son refused to come *home*. And in the long run, the older son was a greater heartache to his father than was the younger son. The younger son, through repentance and faith, received far more from his father than he dared to expect. The older son, because of his unforgiving spirit, insisted that he did not receive what his father owed him.

From this portrait we see that an unforgiving spirit generates bitterness and hostility that results in broken relationships. An unforgiving spirit is dangerous to one's self and to others.

2. Command to Have a Forgiving Spirit (Luke 17:3-4)

One of our greatest tests as Christians comes at this point. Are we to accept God's infinite forgiveness yet fail to offer forgiveness for wrongs done to us by fellow Christians? Are we to harbor bitterness and resentments? No. As Christians, we are commanded to have a forgiving spirit—whether we feel like it or not.

Verses 3-4: **Take heed to yourselves: If thy brother trespass against thee, rebuke him; and if he repent, forgive him. ⁴And if he trespass against thee seven times in a day, and seven times in a day turn again to thee, saying, I repent; thou shalt forgive him.**

The **if** clause is a condition that is not necessarily true, but it could be. **Trespass** in both verses renders the verb for "sin" (*hamartia*). **Against thee** is not in the Greek text of verse 3b, but it is in verse 4. The translation expresses the idea. In such a case, you should **rebuke him.** Instead of telling everyone else about it, face the offending party with it. Speaking your grievance to others will only aggravate the problem. Whatever **thy brother** has done against you, it has hopes of being solved only if you confront the person directly. He may **repent.** If so, **forgive him.**

As a matter of fact, you can forgive in your heart even if the offender does not repent. But that person can only *receive* your forgiveness by repenting and seeking it. God has forgiveness in His heart, else there would have been no offer of salvation in

Christ. "God was in Christ, reconciling the world unto himself" (2 Cor. 5:19; see also Rom. 5:8). Revelation 13:8 refers to Christ as "the Lamb slain from the foundation of the world." That which was a reality in eternity had to be wrought out in time in order that people might believe it and be saved. So forgiveness was in the heart of God before sin was in the hearts of human beings. But for each individual to *receive* this forgiveness, there must be repentance and faith.

How many times should you forgive someone? Jesus used **seven times in a day,** corresponding to repentance seven times a day. In Matthew 18:22 this was the number Peter used. The rabbis taught that forgiveness was required three times. Thus Peter must have thought he was being generous. But Jesus used the figure "until seventy times seven," or 490 times. Should we count up to seven—or even to 490—and stop? Hardly! Jesus was not thinking of arithmetic. In Hebrew numerology seven was considered a perfect number. Any multiple of seven also was a perfect number. So *seven* and *seventy times seven* were perfect or complete numbers. Jesus was thinking of complete or perfect forgiveness—that is, of a forgiving spirit. Christians are to extend unlimited forgiveness to those who have sinned against them.

3. Overcoming an Unforgiving Spirit (Eph. 4:32–5:2)

As believers, we are to forgive one another as God has forgiven us in Christ. But how is such forgiveness possible? It is possible through God's *agape* love working in us. We are to imitate God by living in love. Christ's self-giving is our supreme model of love.

4:32: **And be ye kind one to another, tenderhearted, forgiving one another, even as God for Christ's sake hath forgiven you.**

Christians are to be clothed with certain virtues in personal relationships. **Be** translates the verb "to become" (*ginesthe*). It means "to become what we have not been previously." This will not be achieved in a day. It is a process of becoming. This is seen in the present middle (reflexive) form of the verb. We are to keep on becoming within ourselves. The test of any *process* is the product that results. In a spiritual sense, the *product* is a life in keeping with the very character and nature of God.

Kind expresses the quality that, instead of striking back at evil done, seeks ways of doing good to the evildoer. This virtue is needed within the Christian fellowship. When expressed toward nonbelievers, it bears witness to Christ. **Tenderhearted** expresses compassion as opposed to indifference or even vindictiveness. **Forgiving** (a participle) and **forgiven** (a finite verb) both come from the word for *grace* (*charis*). Thus we could translate it, "gracing one another, even as God in Christ graced you." God does not forgive our sins because of our merits but out of His grace. Likewise, we must forgive others as an act of our grace.

5:1-2: Be ye therefore followers of God, as dear children; ²and walk in love, as Christ also hath loved us, and hath given himself for us an offering and a sacrifice to God for a sweet-smelling savor.

As in 4:32, **be** again translates the verb "to become" (*ginesthe*). **Followers** renders *mimetai*, from which comes our word *mimic*. It means "imitators" (NIV). Christians are to keep on becoming imitators of God as His **dear** (*agapeta*, from *agapetos*, "loved") **children** or "as dearly loved children" (NIV). This is a bold challenge.

Walk renders the verb *peripateo* (note our word *peripatetic*), which means "to walk around." Paul often used this word to express a manner of life. Christians should order their lives **in** [*en*, in the sphere of] **love,** or *agape,* the love that characterizes God's nature. We are to love one another **as Christ also hath loved us.**

Christ gave Himself on our behalf as **an offering and a sacrifice to God. Offering** renders *prosphoran*, from *prosphero*, "to bear to" or "face to face." The verb was used of the priest bearing the sacrifice to present it before God as a sacrifice to Him. Christ's death was an offering to God to satisfy His holy, righteous nature. Christ's death provided the grounds on which God could forgive our sins.

A sweet-smelling savor (see Lev. 4:30-31) is drawn from the offering for the atonement for sin. The *New International Version* reads "as a fragrant offering." In Hebrew thought the aroma of the burnt offering ascended to God. If the aroma was pleasing to God, the offering was accepted. Thus God accepted the sacrifice of His Son as the atonement for our sins.

There is a relationship between the ideas of God's beloved Son and God's beloved children. As the Father accepted (was pleased with) the atoning sacrifice of His Son, He also is pleased when His children give evidence that they belong to Him by living lives characterized by love.

Because God has forgiven us through Christ, we are to cultivate a kind, compassionate, forgiving attitude toward other believers. We are to imitate God and are to follow Christ's model by having a lifestyle characterized by love. Love will exclude an unforgiving spirit.

A story is told about two brothers who were partners in a hardware business and respected leaders in their church. One day, after one of the brothers waited on a customer, he laid the $20 on the cash register with the intention of ringing up the sale in a few minutes. Unfortunately, a telephone call interrupted him, and he needed to go check on an item elsewhere in the store. When he returned, the $20 was gone. The salesman asked his brother where it was. His brother denied any knowledge of what had happened to the money. He said he had not even seen it. After a careful search revealed nothing, inquiry turned to accusation. The brother who made the sale accused the other brother of pocketing the money. Soon harsh words turned to silence, estrangement, and bitter hearts. The distrust and tension between the brothers eventually led to the destruction of their partnership. One brother bought out the other brother's share of the business. That was the last day they spoke to each other. The other brother took his profits and opened a rival hardware store. Everyone in town, it seemed, knew the tragic story of the estranged brothers. This is how the situation stood for 25 years. Then one day a letter arrived in the mail. The writer told how 25 years earlier he was down on his luck and had been walking in the alley behind the hardware store. Seeing the back door open, he looked in. There in plain sight on the cash register was a $20 bill. Seeing no one around, he took the money and hurried off. Now he wanted to apologize and make things right. Enclosed in the envelope was a new, crisp $20 bill.

These brothers held onto their grudge for 25 years! They nursed the imagined and real wrongs in their hearts. They became emotionally and relationally starved. They were psychologically bruised and damaged. And worst of all, they were spiritually crippled by something that should have long since been forgiven and forgotten. Such are the nature and results of an unforgiving spirit.

Each of us should ask ourselves the questions: Which is easier, to forgive someone who has wronged me—especially if that someone is or was dear to me—or to live with the result of cultivating an unforgiving spirit? What wicked memories and bitterness of heart do I hang on to? What is my spirit like?

May God cause each of us to have a forgiving spirit because through Christ God has forgiven us. And may each of us overcome this impediment to spiritual growth.

June 21

APATHY

Background Scripture: Romans 12:11; Revelation 3:14-22
Focal Verses: Romans 12:11; Revelation 3:14-22

INTRODUCTION

1. For many believers there are times in their pilgrimage when they have to ask themselves, How can I recapture my enthusiasm as a Christian?

2. Apathy in the life of a believer is one of the main hindrances to spiritual growth.

3. The Lesson Bible Truth is that Christians are not to become apathetic in Christ's service but are to maintain a productive enthusiasm.

4. The Lesson Outcome is to help you be aware of the pervasiveness and the dangers of spiritual apathy, want to recapture your enthusiasm as a Christian, and commit to strengthen your enthusiasm in Christ's service.

I. SOME PRELIMINARY CONSIDERATIONS

1. The Contemporary Context

Churches, Sunday School classes, Bible study groups, and individual believers seem prone to bouts of apathy. For example, a new Sunday School class is formed with a teacher and a few members. For a time their energy level is high. They reach new members. They serve the Lord. Then at some point the class becomes stagnant and apathetic. The class becomes satisfied with itself or else its energies are expended ministering to its own members to the point that no time or energy is left to enlist new people. Its interests focus inward rather than outward. It reaches a state of the blahs. Eventually stagnation and then decline set in.

Likewise, individual adults may become apathetic and lethargic in their Christian lives. They may become lax in exercising their spiritual gifts and in practicing the disciplines that enable them to grow in their relationship with Christ and in their service for Him. Some believers may have reached a point in their Christian service where they feel they have put in their time and have worked enough. They feel the time has come for someone else to serve. Such adults need to recapture the spiritual enthusiasm that will enable them to continue to grow spiritually.

Apparently the church in Laodicea and its members fell prey to apathy and complacency; hence, the letter it received from the risen Christ.

2. The Biblical Background

Laodicea was a rich center of banking, manufacturing, and trade in the Roman province of Asia (modern-day Turkey). Laodicea was so wealthy that when the city was partially destroyed by an earthquake in A.D. 60, the city was able to rebuild without financial aid from Rome. Its location at the intersection of three Roman highways added to its prominence.

Laodicea also was a sheep-growing center. The raven black wool was in great demand for the manufacture of clothing, carpets, and many other items. In addition, since Laodicea was the center of worship of Asclepius [ask-LAY-pea-uhs], the god of medicine, it was also a great medical center. All these things gave the city a sense of complacency and self-satisfaction. And this attitude affected the spirit of the church there too.

II.   FOCAL VERSES EXAMINED (Rom. 12:11; Rev. 3:14-22)

Romans 12:11 is Paul's exhortation to the Roman Christians to not be apathetic in their Christian service. Revelation 3:14-22 contains the last of the letters the risen Lord wrote to the seven churches in the Roman province of Asia. Laodicea was the only one of the churches in which He found nothing to commend. There was much that He found to condemn, however. The church in Laodicea was marked by compromise and apathy. We would do well to examine ourselves and our churches in light of the things the risen Christ said to this church.

1. Principle (Rom. 12:11)

In Romans 12:11 Paul urged the Roman Christians to maintain their enthusiasm for serving the Lord. He laid down this principle in three brief admonitions.

Verse 11: **Not slothful in business; fervent in spirit; serving the Lord.**

The first admonition, **not slothful in business,** does not have to do with one's employment, vocation, or means of economic livelihood. The word translated **business** (*spoude*) literally means "zeal," "earnestness," "eagerness," "diligence," or "effort." Thus the meaning of this first admonition is better communicated by the *New International Version,* "Never be lacking in zeal," or by the *New Revised Standard Version,* "Do not lag in zeal." The Greek word *okneros,* translated **slothful,** means "lazy" or "complacent." This Greek word was used to describe a person who showed hesitation because of sloth, fear, bashfulness, reserve, or weariness. A. T. Robertson (*Word Pictures in the New Testament,* vol. 4, 404) described such a person as "slow and poky." Since Paul did not specify the object of the "unflagging zeal" (REB) he called for, he must have meant for it to be a general warning. The temptation to lose steam or become complacent is a natural one. As Christians, we have a life-long responsibility to strenuously resist becoming apathetic.

Some Bible students understand Paul's second admonition, **fervent in spirit,** as a warning for Christians to maintain a strong and emotional commitment to the Lord in their own spirits. This is the way the *King James Version* understood the admonition (notice the lower case "s" on **spirit**). The *New International Version* agrees with this interpretation, translating Paul's words "keep your spiritual fervor." The *New Revised Standard Version,* the *New American Standard Bible,* and the *New English Bible* also understand Paul to have been referring to the human spirit. (A parallel example for this view is Acts 18:25, where Apollos was referred to as being "fervent in the spirit.") However, since **spirit** has the definite article in the Greek text (*to pneumati*), and since the parallel in the third admonition in verse 11c refers to the Lord, the reference here probably is to the Holy Spirit. This is the way the *Revised Standard Version,* the *Revised English Bible,* Williams, and the *Contemporary English Version* understand Paul's meaning. **Fervent** translates a word that means "to bubble," "to boil," or "to glow with heat." Paul was exhorting believers to allow themselves to "be aglow with the Spirit" (RSV, REB) or to "be set on fire" by the Holy Spirit.

In the third admonition, **serving** means "to serve as a slave" (*douleuontes*; from *doulos,* a slave). This third admonition does three things. First, it reminds us that as Christians we are to serve. Second, it reminds us that it is **the Lord** we are to serve. Third, it serves as a control on the preceding phrase. James D. G. Dunn ("Romans 9–16," in the *Word Biblical Commentary,* vol. 38a [Dallas: Word Books, 1988], 742) wrote, "'Bubbling with the Spirit' needs always to be checked by and channeled into service of the Lord Christ." Douglas J. Moo (*The Epistle to the Romans,* in The New International Commentary on the New Testament [Grand Rapids: William B. Eerdmans Publishing Company, 1996], 778-779) further cautioned, "The encouragement to be 'set on fire by the Spirit' is, as church history and current experience amply attest, open to abuse. Christians have often been so carried away by enthusiasm for spiritual things that they have left behind those objective standards of Christian living that the Scriptures set forth. This, it seems is Paul's concern; and he seeks to cut off any such abuse by reminding us that being set on fire by the Spirit must lead to, and be directed by, our service of the Lord. It is not the 'enthusiasm' of self-centered display but the enthusiasm of humble service of the Master who bought us that the Spirit creates within us."

Thus, as believers, when we become tired, disillusioned, or discouraged, we need to overcome our apathy and spiritual complacency by never giving up, eagerly following the Holy Spirit, and renewing our enthusiasm for serving the Lord.

2. Problem (Rev. 3:14-17a)

Laodicea has been called a "poor-rich" church. It was rich in potential but poor in spirit and performance. The Laodicean church members were neither hot nor cold but were lukewarm. Their apathy stemmed from their conviction that they were rich and needed nothing.

Christ began this letter in the usual manner. He addressed it and signed it.

Verse 14: **And unto the angel of the church of the Laodiceans write; These things saith the Amen, the faithful and true witness, the beginning of the creation of God.**

Like the other six letters, this letter is addressed to **the angel of the church.** The **angel** of each church probably was the elder or senior pastor who received the letter and was to read it to the church. The risen Christ identified Himself with three expressions: **the Amen, the faithful and true witness, the beginning of the creation of God. The Amen** probably refers to Isaiah 65:16, where Jehovah is called "the God of truth." In this verse the Hebrew word for truth is "amen," so Christ identified Himself as Jehovah. The other designations come from Revelation 1:4-5. The word **witness** is *martus,* the same word as *martyr.* In view of 1:5b-6, Christ probably was called **the faithful and true witness** because of His witness to God's saving love and grace as given in His death on the cross. **The beginning of the creation of God** does not mean that Christ is a created being. The Greek word **beginning** (*arche*) also means "head" or "source." This meaning agrees with John 1:1-3; Colossians 1:15-18; and Hebrews 1:2.

Since the risen Christ found nothing in this church to commend, He immediately moved to His accusation.

Verses 15-17a: **I know thy works, that thou art neither cold nor hot: I would thou wert cold or hot. [16]So then because thou art lukewarm, and neither cold nor hot, I will spew thee out of my mouth. [17a]Because thou sayest, I am rich, and increased with goods, and have need of nothing.**

As with the other churches of Asia Minor that are mentioned in Revelation 2–3, Christ fully knew (*oida*) the **works** of the Laodicean church; but He found two things wrong with it. First, He found this church **neither cold nor hot.** The church at Laodicea was characterized by neither cold indifference nor burning zeal for the Lord's work. It was a self-satisfied church. It was merely **lukewarm**—tepid, insipid, apathetic. Christ wished that it was either **cold or hot,** but He said, **because thou art lukewarm . . . I will spew thee out of my mouth. To spew** renders an infinitive meaning "to vomit" or "to reject with utter disgust." A lukewarm church or a lukewarm believer makes Christ sick to His stomach!

The figure of the lukewarm water probably is drawn from a condition found in Hierapolis [high-uhr-AHP-oh-liss], a nearby city to Laodicea. Beautiful springs of water were there, but they consisted of tepid mineral water. Thirsty travelers would come to these springs expecting to quench their thirst. But when they took the water into their mouths, instead of swallowing it, they would spit or spew it forcefully from their mouths. Hot water stimulates. Cold water refreshes. But tepid water is revolting, especially if it has a strong mineral content. This lukewarm or tepid condition was what the risen Christ found in the church in Laodicea. The church was to have been a Christian oasis in a desert of paganism, but to Christ it was disappointing and disgusting.

Second, Christ found that this Laodicean church, like the city, thought it was economically well off. Again three expressions are used to describe what they thought was their condition: **I am rich, and increased with goods, and have need of nothing. Increased with goods** translates the perfect tense of the verb *plouteo.* Note our word *plutocrat,* a rich person. This church felt that it had no need of anything from either God or man. It had **need of nothing.** It was complacent and completely self-satisfied.

Like this church at Laodicea, Christians will become apathetic in their service for Christ when they feel that they are self-sufficient and secure.

3. Prescription (Rev. 3:17b-22)

The Laodicean believers actually were poverty-stricken and destitute. Jesus counseled them to receive His resources and to repent. When they repented, He would restore fellowship with them. Thus to overcome apathy, believers must realize their condition, repent, and ask Christ to help them see life from His point of view.

Verse 17b: And knowest not that thou art wretched, and miserable, and poor, and blind, and naked.

This church, as some churches today, did not really know its true condition. **Not** renders the strong negative *ouk,* followed by *oidas,* "to have perceptive knowledge." Thus Christ used five words to describe the true condition of this church. **Wretched** renders a word (*talaiporos*) formed from *tlao,* "to endure" or "to bear," and *poros,* "a callus" or a thick, hard place on the skin. Laodicea was a callous church that was totally indifferent to the needs around it. **Miserable** means "pitiful" (NIV). Instead of being an object of pride, it was an object of pity. **Poor** (*ptochos*) indicates absolute poverty, such as that of a beggar—the exact opposite of the rich condition they thought they were in. Here, of course, **poor** refers to spiritual poverty. Furthermore, the church was spiritually **blind** (*tuphlos*) and **naked** (*gymnos*). All of their fine attire could not hide the church's true condition from the Lord.

In the letter to Laodicea, was Christ describing you or your church? We may well imagine that the well-attired congregation in Laodicea experienced a shock wave as it heard the reading of this letter. Did it shock them out of their complacency? their apathy? Did it cause them to burn with indignation? More importantly, what is your reaction to this letter?

In spite of the condition of this church, there was still hope; therefore, Christ exhorted its people to change the situation. As in other matters, He drew on local situations to drive home the spiritual truths. The use of the singular verbs shows that He addressed the individual believers. Whatever the church as a whole might do, each person was responsible for his or her own conduct. As individuals changed, eventually the church would change—for churches are made up of individual believers.

Keeping in mind that Laodicea was the center of the worship of Asclepius [ask-LAY-pea-uhs], the god of medicine, Christ, the Great Physician, prescribed three remedies for this church.

Verse 18: I counsel thee to buy of me gold tried in the fire, that thou mayest be rich; and white raiment, that thou mayest be clothed, and that the shame of thy nakedness do not appear; and anoint thine eyes with eye salve, that thou mayest see.

First, Christ drew on the fact that Laodicea was a banking center. He counseled them **to buy of me gold tried in the fire. Buy** translates a verb based on *agora,* "marketplace"; so Christ told them to go into the marketplace and buy **gold tried in the fire.** This would have been pure gold, not gold mixed with other metallic elements or dross. Or course, the Lord was talking about spiritual values, which constitute true riches.

Second, Christ drew on the background of the popular garments that were made out of the black wool. **White raiment** symbolizes purity and victory. In a city dominated by black garments, those wearing white would stand out. Christians are not to *stand in* with the world but to *stand out* from it.

Third, Christ drew on the fact that Laodicea was famous for its **eye salve,** an ointment used as balm for the eyes. This medicinal salve brought relief to eyes that were inflamed by sun, sand, and hot wind. Christ saw that the Laodicean Christians had been blinded by the glitter of materialism, so He prescribed eye salve in order that they might see. **Mayest see** is a present subjective form. It could be translated "that thou may keep on seeing." They still had some spiritual eyesight, but it needed improving.

Verse 19: As many as I love, I rebuke and chasten: be zealous therefore, and repent.

Christ reminded His readers that He rebukes and chastens in love. **Love** (*philo*) is the warm love of friendship and family relationship. **Chasten** (*paideuo*) renders the verb for the rearing and correction of a child. A parent rebukes and chastens his or her own children. The Laodicean Christians were the Lord's people. He longed to draw them to His bosom, but they needed to be **zealous** and **repent. Be zealous** carries the idea of being on fire or of boiling. They were to be boiling hot for the Lord and His work, not tepid or apathetic. **Repent** translates a verb meaning "a change of mind." To the Greeks, the mind referred to the whole person—so this means a complete change of life was needed.

Verse 20: **Behold, I stand at the door, and knock: if any man hear my voice, and open the door, I will come in to him, and will sup with him, and he with me.**

This verse often has been used in evangelistic invitations. But in the context, the risen Lord was knocking on the door of an indifferent, apathetic church—or of indifferent, apathetic Christians' hearts—seeking entrance so it might have a vital spiritual fellowship with Him.

"The verb **stand** renders a perfect tense of completeness. Christ is always there. **Knock** renders a present tense—keep on knocking. So 'I am constantly standing at the door and keeping on knocking.' Both **hear** and **open** are aorist subjunctives. There is the possibility that at any time any one may hear and open. But it is not certain that it will be true" (Herschel H. Hobbs, *The Cosmic Drama* [Waco: Word Books, 1971], 64).

While Christ does the knocking, we must **open the door.** God takes the initiative, but each person must respond positively. **Sup with him,** or "eat with him" (NIV), is in contrast to the nausea mentioned in verses 15-16.

Verses 21-22 show that faithfulness to Christ has both temporal as well as eternal benefits.

Verses 21-22: **To him that overcometh will I grant to sit with me in my throne, even as I also overcame, and am set down with my Father in his throne. [22]He that hath an ear, let him hear what the Spirit saith unto the churches.**

Here is the promise of reward and glory in heaven for eternity. After Christ had been victorious in His redemptive mission, He sat down **with my Father in his throne.** To His victorious people Christ gives the right to sit with Him in His throne (see also Luke 22:28-30; Rev. 22:5).

The words of verse 22 are found in each of the seven letters to the churches of Asia. Congregations and individuals are to listen to the Spirit's voice that accompanies the words of Jesus. This concluding exhortation provides a warning about apathy as well as a word of challenge and encouragement.

When it comes to apathy, we can't afford to be like the wag who said, "Apathy. I'm neither for it nor against it." Nor can we be like the university student whose professor noticed him nodding off during class. The teacher called on him and asked, "Which is the greater problem in our society—ignorance or apathy?" The student yawned and replied, "I don't know, and I don't care."

Don't let apathy—or ignorance either for that matter—hinder your spiritual growth.

SELF-CENTEREDNESS

Background Scripture: Philippians 2:19-24;
James 3:13-16; 1 John 2:15-17
Focal Verses: Philippians 2:19-24; James 3:13-16;
1 John 2:15-17

INTRODUCTION

1. How many times have you heard it said, "If you don't look out for yourself, neither will anybody else"?
2. This raises the question, What's wrong with looking out for number one?
3. The Lesson Bible Truth is that Christians are to strive to remove selfish ambition from their lives and to consider others' interests.
4. The Lesson Outcome is to help you recognize your tendency toward self-centeredness, want to become more self-giving, and decide ways you will become more self-giving.

I. SOME PRELIMINARY CONSIDERATIONS

1. The Contemporary Context

Many adults struggle with the tendency to become self-centered. People too easily can become focused on themselves—their ambitions, needs, desires, interests, comfort, and security. They can become self-serving, grasping, greedy. They can concentrate more on having others serve them than on serving people. Their self-absorption can cause them to treat others as objects to be manipulated rather than as persons of worth to be valued and affirmed. Self-centered adults need to be made aware or reminded that genuine love is not selfish but has a genuine interest in others' welfare. Self-centeredness is a hindrance to spiritual growth; self-giving is both evidence of and a means to spiritual growth.

2. The Biblical Background

Near the end of the first century, the apostle John wrote his first epistle to believers in the circle of churches that he was familiar with and warned them not to allow their self-centered desires and selfish ambition for what the world had to offer to hinder their spiritual growth. When James, the brother of our Lord, wrote his epistle about A.D. 50 to Jewish Christians who were scattered outside of Palestine, he drew a contrast between self-centered earthly wisdom, which generates envy and selfish ambition and results in disorder and evil practices, and divine wisdom, which is unselfish and other-centered and issues in a lifestyle marked by good deeds done in humility. When Paul wrote his letter to the Philippians from prison in Rome about A.D. 61, he pointed to Timothy as an example of one who was not self-centered and who did not look out only for his own interests.

II. FOCAL VERSES EXAMINED
(Phil. 2:19-24; Jas. 3:13-16; 1 John 2:15-17)

The Scripture passages for this lesson will be studied in the order of the points made in the lesson rather than in their canonical order.

1. Contrast of Two Ways (1 John 2:15-17)

In 1 John 2:15-17 John contrasted two types of people and the outcomes of their lives—those whose lives are self-centered and those whose lives are God-centered.

Verse 15: **Love not the world, neither the things that are in the world. If any man love the world, the love of the Father is not in him.**

The **world** itself is not inherently evil. It is God's world. He created it, and He pronounced it good (Gen. 1:1,31). The same is true of **the things that are in the world.** When used within the will of God, **the things that are in the world** are for our blessing. But here in verses 15-17 John used the word **world** (*kosmos*) six times to connote a social order that takes no thought of God and has no place for Him in its system. **The things that are in the world** are defined by verse 16. The world and the things of the world cater to our fleshly human natures. The world and its values are contrary to God.

When John commanded **love not the world,** he used the verb *agapate* for **love,** a word that carries the idea of absolute loyalty to its object. The devil seeks to pervert this beautiful, noble quality into something evil. Preceded by the negative particle *me,* we could translate this present, active, imperative verb as "Stop loving the world" or "Do not have the habit of loving the world." We are not to give absolute loyalty to the world or the things in it. Such loyalty belongs only to God. You cannot give absolute loyalty both to God and to the world. God and the world are mutually exclusive. John concluded that if anyone loves the world, **the love of** God **the Father is not in him.**

Verse 16: For all that is in the world, the lust of the flesh, and the lust of the eyes, and the pride of life, is not of the Father, but is of the world.

Verse 16 defines what **all that is in the world** means. Three phrase are used: **the lust of the flesh, the lust of the eyes,** and **the pride of life. Lust** (*epithumia*), used in the first two expressions, expresses desires or cravings. **The flesh** (*sarkos*) here is used in an ethical sense to refer to the sinful nature, not to the physical body. The *New International Version* reads, "the cravings of sinful man." Thus **the lust of the flesh** refers to an outlook that is orientated toward self, that self-sufficiently pursues its own ends independent of God.

The lust of the eyes can refer to sexual lust; to everything and anything that is outward, visible, showy, and enticing to the eyes; or to the greed and desire for things that are aroused by seeing them.

For the third phrase we might have expected a third *epithumia*—"the lust for riches and wealth." But John "had his sights set on a more serious vice than the ostentation of the wealthy or their arrogance toward the poor. He contrasts with God the creaturely pride, the mastery of one's own existence, of the person who decides and directs the course of his life without taking God into account. This 'sufficiency' is the exact opposite of the absolute duty of worshiping God and serving God devoutly" (Ceslas Spicq, "*Alazoneia, alazon,*" in the *Theological Lexicon of the New Testament,* vol. 1 [Peabody, MA: Hendrickson Publishers, Inc., 1996], 65). Thus the third phrase is **the pride of life.** In this expression the word **pride** is *alazoneia* and the word for **life** is *bios.* Both of these words are important. Appropriately, the word John used for **life** was *bios,* physical life or the animal principle of life, not *zoe,* spiritual life or salvation life. *Zoe* denotes eternal life, but *bios* expresses temporary life that passes away. Only here and in James 4:16 is the noun form of the word for **pride** (*alazoneia*) used in the New Testament. The adjective *alazon* is used in Romans 1:30 and 2 Timothy 3:2. This word means "boaster" or "braggart." It refers to "boasting with arrogant words" or "boastful presumption." It "describes a pretentious hypocrite who glories in himself or in his possessions" (Glenn W. Barker, "1 John," in *The Expositor's Bible Commentary,* vol. 12 [Grand Rapids: Zondervan Publishing House, 1981], 322). Edward A. McDowell ("1-2-3 John," in *The Broadman Bible Commentary,* vol. 12 [Nashville: Broadman Press, 1972], 202) wrote, "Pride here is braggadocio, empty talk, the foolish presumption of one who trusts in his own resources and disdains the power of God and the rights of others." Thus the *New International Version* rightly translates **the pride of life** as "the boasting of what he has and does."

Plutarch (A.D. 50–120), the ancient Greek philosopher, moralist, and biographer—who was a contemporary of John—described "the *Alazon*" in his *Characters.* "The *Alazon* is the kind of person who will stand on the mole and tell perfect strangers what a lot of money he has at sea, and discourse of his investments, how large they are, and what gains and losses he has made, and as he spins his yarns he will send his boy to the bank—his balance being a shilling. If he enjoys company on the road, he is apt to tell how he served with Alexander the Great, how he got on with him, and how many jewelled cups he brought home; and to discuss the Asiatic craftsmen, how much

better they are than any in Europe—never having been away
from Athens. He will say that he was granted a free permit for
the export of timber, but took no advantage of it, to avoid ill-
natured gossip; and that during the corn-shortage he spent
more than fifteen hundred pounds in gifts to needy citizens. He
will be living in a rented house, and will tell anyone who does
not know the facts that this is the family residence, but he is
going to sell it because it is too small for his entertainments"
(quoted in Barker, "1 John," 322, from C. H. Dodd, *The Johan-
nine Epistles,* in the Moffatt New Testament Commentary
[London: Hodder and Stoughton, 1946], 42).

**Verse 17: And the world passeth away, and the lust
thereof: but he that doeth the will of God abideth forever.**

So many people live self-centered lives, desiring and acquiring
things they can see and touch. But all the things of the world are
temporary, transitory; they "are passing away"—a present tense
verb showing linear action. Even as John wrote these words, the
world was passing away; it already was putrefying—"a corpse
not yet buried" (Barker, "1 John," 322).

One who lives a self-centered life, one whose life is driven by
the lust of the flesh, the lust of the eye, or what he has and
does, lives only for passing pleasures. The passions of youth
fade with old age. And material possessions, of which one could
boast, can be lost in a day. Certainly at death all of one's material possessions must be left behind. By way of contrast, the one
who does **the will of God** "keeps on abiding"—a present active
participle—**forever,** or "unto the age" (*eis ton aiona*). Those
who live for God and His will have age-abiding life.

Self-centeredness and selfish ambition hinder spiritual
growth. As believers, we must guard against allowing desires for
what the world offers to take priority over doing God's will and
loving Him.

2. Results of Self-Centeredness (Jas. 3:13-16)

James drew a contrast between divine wisdom and earthly
wisdom. Earthly wisdom is self-centered. It generates envy and

selfish ambition that result in disorder and evil practices. Divine wisdom is unselfish and other-centered. It issues in a lifestyle marked by good deeds done in humility.

Verse 13: Who is a wise man and endued with knowledge among you? let him show out of a good conversation his works with meekness of wisdom.

First, James focused on the one who lives by divine wisdom. The Greek text reads as the *New International Version* translates it, "Who is wise and understanding among you?" **Wise** (*sophos*) was the technical term among the Jews for a teacher, scribe, or rabbi. The term **knowledge** (*epistemon*), or "understanding," was used to describe one who was an expert, one who had special knowledge or training, "a skilled and scientific person with a tone of superiority" (Robertson, *Word Pictures in the New Testament,* vol. 6, 45). James's interrogative, **Who** (*tis*), was rhetorical. He did not expect an answer. He used a rhetorical question to present an exhortation. He said, in effect, "Show it by the way you live." **Conversation** means "the manner in which you live." The obsolete use of the English word refers to one's *conduct,* not merely to one's *conversation.* The wise person is known by how he or she *lives,* not merely by what he or she *says.* The wise person's life is characterized by **good** conduct and by **works.** Such **works** are done in the **meekness of wisdom. Meekness** does not mean weakness; **meekness** (*prauteti*) means "teachableness." The *New International Version* renders it "humility." A better translation might be "gentleness" (NRSV, NASB). The Greek word *prautes* was used of a horse that had been broken and trained to submit to a bridle. Hence it pictures strength under control.

Verses 14-16: But if ye have bitter envying and strife in your hearts, glory not, and lie not against the truth. [15]This wisdom descendeth not from above, but is earthly, sensual, devilish. [16]For where envying and strife is, there is confusion and every evil work.

Next, James focused on those who live by earthly wisdom. These verses are in direct contrast to verse 13. **But** (*de*) is an adversative, setting verses 14-16 over against verse 13. James went to the heart of the matter, focusing on two self-centered attitudes. The key word is **strife** (*eritheian*). The *New International Version* translates this word "selfish ambition." According to Robertson, this word denotes "a pushing forward for personal ends, partisanship" (*Word Pictures in the New Testament*, vol. 6, 46). Donald W. Burdick stated that the Greek word "speaks of a self-seeking attitude bent on gaining advantage and prestige for oneself" ("James," in *The Expositor's Bible Commentary*, vol. 12 [Grand Rapids: Zondervan Publishing House, 1981], 190). In other words, James was talking about self-centeredness.

Envying renders *zelon*, from which we get our word *zeal*. Literally, the Greek word means "to burn" or "to boil." Depending on the context, this word may be used in a good (John 2:17) or bad (Acts 5:17) sense. Here in verses 14 and 16 it is colored by its association with **strife,** or "selfish ambition," and with the modifying term **bitter** (*pikron*); so it is used in the bad sense of "selfish zeal."

The so-called **wisdom** that is expressed in self-centeredness and selfish ambition is not from heaven. Rather, it is **earthly, sensual,** and **devilish. Earthly** refers to its source as well as its kind. It views life and adopts its values from the world's viewpoint rather than from God's viewpoint and values. Its mind is set on earthly things (Phil. 3:19). **Sensual** the *New International Version* translates as "unspiritual." The Greek word is *psychike* (note our word *psychology*). In 1 Corinthians 2:14-15 Paul contrasted the carnal or unspiritual person (*psychikos*) with the spiritual person (*pneumatikos*). The spiritual person (*pneumatikos*) is spiritual because he or she has received the Spirit of God. The unspiritual person (*psychikos*) is devoid of the Spirit of God (Jude 19). Thus wisdom that is sensual or unspiritual (*psychikos*) characterizes the unregenerate nature. It arises out of our fallen human nature. Finally, it also is **devilish** or "of the devil" (NIV). Literally, James said it is "demonic" (*daimoniodes*).

The results of self-centeredness and selfish ambition are **confusion** and **evil work** or "disorder and every evil practice"

(NIV). **Confusion** (*akatastasia*), or "disorder" (NIV), is a common Greek term for anarchy and political turmoil (Luke 21:9). **Evil work** refers to worthless activity and deeds that are good for nothing.

Make no mistake about it, self-centeredness, selfish zeal, and selfish ambition always tend to destroy spiritual life, spiritual growth, and spiritual work. Self-centeredness is a major hindrance to spiritual growth.

3. Example of Unselfishness (Phil. 2:19-24)

In contrast to people who were self-centered and who looked out only for their own interests, Timothy genuinely was interested in the Philippian believers' welfare. He had proved himself in Christian service. Hence Paul sent Timothy to the Philippian Christians.

Verses 19-24: **But I trust in the Lord Jesus to send Timotheus shortly unto you, that I also may be of good comfort, when I know your state. [20]For I have no man likeminded, who will naturally care for your state. [21]For all seek their own, not the things which are Jesus Christ's. [22]But ye know the proof of him, that, as a son with the father, he hath served with me in the gospel. [23]Him therefore I hope to send presently, so soon as I shall see how it will go with me. [24]But I trust in the Lord that I also myself shall come shortly.**

Paul was anxious to receive word from Philippi about the Philippian believers' situation. He wanted an up-to-date report on his friends. Such a report would bring Paul **good comfort** or "cheer." This verb (*eupsycho*) occurs only here in the New Testament. Paul planned to send **Timotheus** (that is, Timothy) to Philippi so he could bring Paul the latest news of the church there. Timothy, however, would wait to find out what was the result of Paul's appearance at Caesar's tribunal before he left on his journey (**so soon as I shall see how it will go with me).** Paul himself hoped to visit them **shortly,** indicating he was expecting a favorable verdict from the court.

Paul said that no one was more **likeminded** to him concerning the Philippians than Timothy. The word *isopsychon,* used only here in the New Testament, means "of like soul" or "of like mind." Possibly Paul meant that he had "no one of a mind equal to Timothy"; but, in fact, Paul said he had no one else to send—**for all seek their own, not the things which are Jesus Christ's.** Obviously Paul did not mean to include Luke or Aristarchus [ehr-iss-TAHR-kuhs], who probably were away on missions elsewhere, or Epaphroditus [ih-paf-roh-DIGH-tuhs], who brought the gift to Paul from the church at Philippi at the risk of his own life.

Apparently self-centeredness was a problem in the early church as well! Timothy had been with Paul on his first visit to Philippi and was not only well-known in the church at Philippi but, Paul wrote, Timothy **naturally care**[s] **for your state;** that is, Timothy "takes a genuine interest in your welfare" (NIV). There was proof of this, and they knew it—**But ye know the proof of him. Proof** translates *dokimen,* "proof after being tested." He already had stood the test in his concern for the Philippians and in his loyalty to Paul. **As a son with the father,** Timothy had **served with** Paul (**with me,** *syn emoi*) **in the** furtherance of the **gospel.** Timothy had earned his spurs. No longer was he Paul's helper; he was his partner in the work.

Timothy is a good example of spiritual growth. He was not self-centered. He served others and looked out for the welfare of others, not for his own. When we do that, we too will grow spiritually. When we as believers overcome our self-centeredness and have a genuine interest in the welfare of other people, we will receive greater responsibilities and have greater opportunities to serve the Lord.

And so, in the words of verse 21, let me ask you a question. Do you seek your own things or the things that are Jesus Christ's? What are you doing to overcome the spiritual hindrance of self-centeredness in your life?

STUDY THEME: BEING A PEACEMAKER

July 5

HONOR GOD

Background Scripture: Philippians 2:1-11; 4:2-9
Focal Verses: Philippians 2:1-5; 4:2-9

INTRODUCTION

1. This week's lesson begins a new four-lesson study theme titled "Being a Peacemaker."

2. Disagreements, controversy, conflict, and litigation abound in our society. Unfortunately, these appear among God's people as well. Often it seems easier to ignore or deny conflict situations, escape from them, or react to them with attack responses rather than to promote genuine peace by restoring broken relationships and seeking change in constructive ways.

3. The four lessons in this study theme are designed to help you learn biblical principles of resolving personal conflict and feel the need to resolve personal conflicts in light of God's Word so that you will be a peacemaker.

4. God's Word, the Bible, offers peacemaking principles that are effective in today's complicated society and in our personal lives. Four essentials of peacemaking that are revealed in God's Word are identified, explained, and illustrated in these lessons. According to Christian attorney Ken Sande, the executive director of Peacemaker Ministries, these principles center in four "G's": *G*lorify God, *G*et the Log Out of Your Eye, *G*o and Show Your Brother His Fault, and *G*o and Be Reconciled (*The Peacemaker: A Biblical Guide to Resolving Personal Conflict,* 2nd ed. [Grand Rapids: Baker Book House, 1997], 10-11). This first lesson focuses on glorifying or honoring God.

5. You may have wondered, *How can I please and honor God in conflict situations?*

6. The Lesson Bible Truth is that conflict situations provide opportunities to please and honor God.

7. The Lesson Outcome is to help you develop a desire and commitment to please and honor God in conflict situations.

I. SOME PRELIMINARY CONSIDERATIONS

1. God and Conflict

When people experience conflict, honoring God seldom enters their minds. When people fail to focus on God, they are more likely to respond to conflict in a self-centered, impulsive, and adversarial manner. Too often Christians and churches set a poor example of honoring God in conflict situations.

2. The Biblical Background

Paul's Epistle to the Philippians is a thank-you letter for money the Philippian church sent to Paul during his first Roman imprisonment (about A.D. 61). Epaphroditus [eh-paf-row-DIE-tuss] delivered the church's gift. Epaphroditus also brought news of a conflict situation within the church fellowship in Philippi. Paul sought to deal with this problem from far-away Rome.

The conflict within the Christian fellowship posed a great danger in that it threatened to shatter the church fellowship. So the apostle proceeded to deal with the problem. As we examine Paul's procedure, we would do well to consider the suggestions Paul made to help them resolve their conflict as Christians.

II. FOCAL VERSES EXAMINED (Phil. 2:1-5; 4:2-9)

In 2:1-4 Paul called on his readers to solve their conflict through unity of purpose and self-abnegation. They were to refuse to let personal interest or position control the course of their lives. He summed this up in verse 5 with a plea that they have the mind of Christ. In 4:2-9 Paul addressed two women in the church who were experiencing conflict with each other.

1. Imitate Christ (Phil. 2:1-5)

Paul first spoke positively (vv. 1-2), then negatively (vv. 3-4).

Verse 1: **If there be therefore any consolation in Christ, if any comfort of love, if any fellowship of the Spirit, if any bowels and mercies.**

Paul began his exhortation to Christian unity in verse 1 by naming four incentives. The Greek construction of the four **if** clauses shows they were assumed to be true. We could translate them "since." First, Paul pointed out, as Christians, they were in a vital union with Christ. The meaning of the words **if there be therefore any consolation in Christ** is clearer when they are translated "if you have any encouragement from being united with Christ" (NIV). The second incentive Paul cited that should encourage Christians to overcome conflict among themselves was the **comfort of love.** Believers' love for Christ and their love for each other ought to impel them to desist from all divisiveness and conflict. A third incentive was the **fellowship** produced by the Holy **Spirit.** This should stimulate unity and dispel conflict. What the *King James Version* translates as **bowels and mercies** is the fourth incentive. Much as we would refer to the *heart* today, in biblical psychology the *splanchna,* or **bowels,** were the seat of the affections, the seat of one's innermost feelings. The *New International Version* translates the words of this fourth incentive, "if any tenderness and compassion." That is, the tenderness and compassion among the believers should make unity and not conflict the normal and expected thing.

Verses 2-4: **Fulfill ye my joy, that ye be likeminded, having the same love, being of one accord, of one mind. ³Let nothing be done through strife or vainglory; but in lowliness of mind let each esteem other better than themselves. ⁴Look not every man on his own things, but every man also on the things of others.**

Since these four things were true, then a certain attitude and conduct should follow. Thus Paul strongly urged (imperative mood) them to "complete" (NIV) or **fulfill**—that is, to "fill full"—

his **joy** by being **likeminded** in thought and action. Paul explained how they could do this in four participial phrases.

First, they were to possess a mutual love, **having the same love** (v. 2). Second, they were to set their minds on unity with oneness of soul, **being of one accord, of one mind. Of one accord** renders a Greek word meaning "to be knit or joined together in soul." Third, they were to avoid selfish ambition and conceit and humbly consider others above themselves. **Lowliness of mind** translates one Greek word. This particular word is not found in nonbiblical Greek. The verb form was used in the Greek translation of the Old Testament (called the Septuagint) in the sense of "pious humility." To the Greeks, humility was a negative characteristic; but the New Testament writers transformed it into a positive virtue. **Lowliness of mind,** or "humility" (NIV), is the mind-set of one who truly recognizes his or her unworthiness before the Lord. Fourth, they were to look not only to their own interests but also to the interests of others. **But . . . also** indicates that we should not neglect or ignore our own interests and affairs to involve ourselves in the good of others. Rather, it teaches us that the interests and affairs of other believers are also to form a part of our concerns. The *New International Version* brings this out clearer: "Each of you should look not only to your own interests, but also to the interests of others."

Selfish ambition, personal prestige, and concentration on self inevitably produce strife and factions as each person seeks to further himself or herself at the expense of others. Out of such, conflict among believers and church splits are made.

Verse 5: **Let this mind be in you, which was also in Christ Jesus.**

With this verse Paul introduced his supreme example of humility and self-abnegation, **Christ Jesus.** Paul's desire was that all saints have this **mind** or "attitude" (NIV). That is, Paul desired that they forget themselves in serving others, and that they leave recognition and reward with God. The **you** is plural (*humin*). Paul wrote to the church collectively, but each individual believer should have the same attitude as Christ.

Christians in conflict situations honor God when they imitate Christ by acting in humility and looking out for the interests of others.

2. Agree in the Lord (Phil. 4:2-3)

When he addressed two of his friends who were in conflict, "Paul implicitly reminds the women that their conflict provides an opportunity to glorify God, to serve others, and to grow to be like Christ. He also emphasizes the importance of peace and unity in God's kingdom, and he says that Euodia and Syntyche should receive help from the church if they cannot resolve their dispute privately. Most importantly, he reminds them that God is intimately involved in their situation and able to help them resolve it" (Sande, *The Peacemaker,* 74).

Verses 2-3: **I beseech Euodias, and beseech Syntyche, that they be of the same mind in the Lord. [3]And I entreat thee also, true yokefellow, help those women which labored with me in the gospel, with Clement also, and with other my fellow laborers, whose names are in the book of life.**

The double use of **beseech** in verse 2 may indicate that each of the women Paul addressed needed a separate admonition because the discord between them had become so great. Paul did not seek to tell them what to do; he made a plea. **Euodias** [yoo-OH-dee-uhs] ("Euodia" in the NIV) means "prosperous journey" (*eu,* "good," and *hodos,* "road"). **Syntyche** [SIN-ti-kee] means "pleasant acquaintance" or "good luck" (Robertson, *Word Pictures in the New Testament,* vol. 4, 458). If only these women had lived up to their names! Paul pleaded with them to be **of the same mind in the Lord.** Whatever the problem was, if each of them would allow their attitudes to be formed in the Lord, the disharmony between these two women would disappear. Similarly, when Christians today experience conflict with other believers, they need to recall their common bond in Christ and allow that relationship to help them find agreement.

Paul did not spell out the problem between these two women, but he used an important strategy in conflict situations. He

called on a third party to help mediate in the dispute. **I entreat thee also, true yokefellow, help those women. Yokefellow** is the Greek word *syzygus*. Bible students debate two
questions about Paul's appeal. First, was Paul referring to a
person by the name of *Syzygus* or was this word a descriptive
moniker? *The New Jerusalem Bible*, for example, understands
the word as a proper name. It reads, "I ask you, Syzygus, really
to be 'partner' and help them" (similarly, *The Jerusalem Bible*).
Second, if Paul was not referring to an individual by the name
of Syzygus, then who was Paul referring to as the **true** or
"loyal" (NIV) **yokefellow** (*gnesie syzyge*)? Many suggestions
have been made—including the husband or brother of Euodias
or Syntyche, Epaphroditus, Timothy, Silas, Luke, the pastor of
the church, the chief bishop at Philippi, Lydia, and Christ Himself. Some interpreters have found it strange that Paul suddenly would address a single individual in a letter otherwise
addressed to a whole church. These Bible students think Paul
was addressing the Christian church as a unit. That is, the
Philippian believers—as if they were a single individual—were
to help these women resolve their conflict and reconcile their
differences. Either way, Paul exhorted this believer—or the
Philippian church—to live up to this name.

Even the verb Paul chose for **help,** "assist," or "aid" (*syllam-
banou*) implies unity of effort. The compound Greek word is a
combination of *syn*, "with," and *lambano*, "to take hold of." In
other words, the "loyal friend" was to "take hold with someone
in order to provide the needed assistance." In fact, Paul used
five words compounded with the Greek preposition "with" (*syn*)
in verses 2-3, indicating a subtle though powerful stress on the
importance of third party intervention in helping to resolve conflict situations and restore unity and harmony. People who are
in conflict situations often need a third party to help bring about
reconciliation between those on the two sides of the issue.

Paul then listed an important reason for helping Euodias and
Syntyche resolve their differences—these two women had
worked with Paul and others in the furtherance of the gospel.
What Paul actually wrote is stronger than the *King James Ver-*

sion's **labored with me in the gospel.** The Greek word translated **labored with me** or "contended at my side" (NIV) literally is "fought together side-by-side with." The Greek word
synathlein is drawn from the gladiatorial arena or the games. It
is used only here and in 1:27 in the New Testament. "It implies
a united struggle in preaching the gospel, on the one hand, and
a sharing in the sufferings that results from the struggle, on the
other" (Gerald F. Hawthorne, "Philippians," in the *Word Biblical
Commentary,* vol. 43 [Waco: Word Books, 1983], 180). These
woman had been part of Paul's team. They were his coworkers
in spreading the gospel, equal with **Clement** and "the rest of
the workers with me" (*ton loipon synergon mou*), that is, the others who fought side-by-side with Paul in spreading the gospel.
Even though Paul did not mention the names of his **other fellow laborers,** he knew they were not forgotten, for their names
were recorded in the **book of life**—the heavenly record of all
believers. This does not necessarily imply that they had died,
only that they were secure as believers. Thus we are reminded
that when believers have unresolved disagreements with each
other, they become distracted and divert resources and energy
away from the Lord's work.

3. Trust in God (Phil. 4:4-7)

Paul did not proceed to instruct Euodias and Syntyche about
every action they should take to resolve their conflict. Instead,
he focused on the principles they needed to learn to develop a
proper attitude toward their situation and toward each other. In
doing so, Paul suggested five basic principles that are "an excellent formula for examining one's attitudes during a conflict"
(Sande, *The Peacemaker,* 74-75). Paul's first principle was **rejoice in the Lord always.**

Verses 4-5: **Rejoice in the Lord always: and again I say,
Rejoice. ⁵Let your moderation be known unto all men.
The Lord is at hand.**

As usual, Paul urged these Philippian believers to be God-
centered in their approach to conflict. Furthermore, he wanted

them to be joyfully God-centered—**Rejoice in the Lord always.** And, in case they missed it the first time or wanted to skip over this point, Paul repeated it for emphasis—**and again I say, Rejoice.**

What was there that these believers could rejoice about when they were involved in a dispute? To begin with, they could rejoice over having received forgiveness through Christ. The more they rejoiced in that forgiveness, the easier it would be for them to forgive one another. Furthermore, they could rejoice over the fact that God had given them the church to guide, strengthen, and support them.

Paul's second principle in developing a proper attitude toward conflict was to **let your moderation be known unto all men. Moderation** (*epieikes*) translates a word that means "gentleness" (NIV) or "sweet reasonableness." Other English terms that help explain the meaning of the original Greek word are "yielding," "forbearing," "lenient," "magnanimous," "kind," "considerate," "courteous," "large-hearted," and "generous." This Greek word (*epieikes*) points to the attitude of showing consideration and kindness to others and being willing to yield one's own personal rights. It describes a quality that is the opposite of irritability, rudeness, and abrasiveness. It describes a quality that would make a person *nice* instead of *nasty.* Such an attitude is necessary in resolving conflict. Paul said that this quality was to **be known,** "displayed toward," or "seen and recognized by" **all men.** The *New International Version* reads, "Let your gentleness be evident to all." It's easy to display gentleness toward some people, but Paul exhorted the Philippians to display it toward **all** (*pasin*) people.

"Being gentle in the midst of conflict produces several benefits, especially when it is 'evident to all.' It reflects Christ's presence and power in your life, which pleases and honors him. It also guards you from speaking and acting harshly, which would only make matters worse. Finally, your gentleness may encourage similar behavior in your opponent" (Sande, *The Peacemaker,* 76).

The basis on which they should rejoice and on which they should let their gentleness be evident to all was their expectancy with regard to the Lord's return. **At hand** renders *engus,* which is ambiguous. The expression covers *near in space* as well as *near in time.* Thus **the Lord is at hand** could mean that the Lord is near or close to you, aware of your conduct, and concerned with your attitude. Or it could mean that Jesus Christ's return is imminent. This view is represented in *Today's English Version, the Contemporary English Version, The Living Bible, the New Living Translation,* and the *New Century Version,* among others. If this is what Paul meant, then he was indicating that it would be easier to put up with harassment and to demonstrate magnanimity if they kept the thought "The Lord is coming soon" in front of them. After all, they would not want the Lord to find the church in Philippi in conflict—even though the Lord knew about it all the time. Being joyful and tolerant toward others, even those who delight in causing conflict, is evidence of an attitude that comes from living the peace of God.

Verses 6-7: **Be careful for nothing; but in everything by prayer and supplication with thanksgiving let your requests be made known unto God. ⁷And the peace of God, which passeth all understanding, shall keep your hearts and minds through Christ Jesus.**

Paul's third principle in developing a godly attitude toward conflict was to get rid of anxious thoughts and replace that anxiety with prayer.

Be careful for nothing suggests a happy-go-lucky attitude toward life. This is *not* what Paul meant. The Greek verb *merimnao* means "to be divided in mind," "to be overly anxious," "to be laden with cares and troubles," "to be pressured," "to be squeezed," "to be burdened," or "to be under stress." "These feelings tend to multiply when we are in the middle of a dispute, especially if it involves a person who is very important to us or if valuable interests are at stake" (Sande, *The Peacemaker,* 76). The *New International Version* reads, "Do not be anxious about anything."

Paul went on to say that praying to God cures anxiety. The way to avoid being overanxious about anything is through prayer. Paul used three words for talking to God. **Prayer** denotes a worshipful attitude. **Supplication** or "petition" (NIV) is prayer that expresses needs. And **requests** refers to those things that are asked for. Paul told God's people to make their requests **known unto God.** These prayers and petitions should be presented with **thanksgiving** for what God already has done and for what He will do in the future.

The result of focusing on God through prayer will be that God's peace will **keep your hearts and minds through Christ Jesus. Keep** renders a military term that means "to guard" or "to garrison." God's peace is described further as that **which passeth all understanding.** "When God works in his people, things begin to happen that don't make sense to the world" (Sande, *The Peacemaker,* 77).

And so we see that in conflict situations, Christians demonstrate their trust in God and experience His peace when they rejoice in Him, show a gentle spirit, and replace their anxiety with prayer.

4. Pursue Excellence (Phil. 4:8-9)

Paul's fourth principle toward developing a proper attitude during a conflict is to see things as they really are. This means developing a more accurate view of your opponent. "If you respond to conflict like most people, you will tend to focus on the negative characteristics of the person who is disagreeing with you, exaggerating faults and overlooking virtues. The more distorted your perspective becomes, the more likely you are to imagine the worst about your opponent, which may lead you to misjudge completely his or her values, motives, and actions. A negative perspective usually also leads to bitterness, to dwelling on your hurt and thinking how undeserving of it you are. The best way to overcome this prejudicial tendency is to think deliberately about aspects of your opponent that are true, noble, right, pure, lovely, admirable—in short, 'excellent, or praiseworthy.'" (Sande, *The Peacemaker,* 77-78).

Verse 8: **Finally, brethren, whatsoever things are true, whatsoever things are honest, whatsoever things are**

just, whatsoever things are pure, whatsoever things are lovely, whatsoever things are of good report; if there be any virtue, and if there be any praise, think on these things.

Paul used **finally** to mark the conclusion of the matter of peace. If the Philippian Christians had a wholesome thought atmosphere, it would be conducive to the working of God's peace. The second person plural form of the verb rendered **think** shows that Paul had all of his readers in mind. Through unified thought they could submit themselves to God and thus know His peace.

Each virtue has its own verb; thus each stands on its own. **True** (*alethe*) means "truthfulness" or "dependability." **Honest** (*semna*) may read "honorable" or "noble" (NIV). **Just** (*dikaia*) or "right" (NIV) means "giving to God and people a justness that is worthy of them." **Pure** (*hagna*) renders a word that refers to "being holy or pure in relation to God." It is used of clean things such as thoughts, words, or deeds. **Lovely** (*prosphile*) means "that which calls forth love." It also refers to that which is "pleasing" and "winsome." **Good report** (*euphema*) means "speaking well of something." The *New International Version* reads "admirable." **Virtue** (*arete*) denotes moral excellence. **Praise** (*epainos*) refers to something that is "praiseworthy" (NIV), such as God.

When Paul came to **if there be any,** he suddenly changed his structure to a conditional clause. This is a rhetorical device that forced his readers to exercise their own discernment about the things that are morally excellent and praiseworthy. Then he told them to **think on these things.**

We are responsible for our thoughts. We should have the habit of thinking (present imperative) high, noble thoughts, for what we think will soon become our actions. If we think right thoughts, we will perform right actions. Conversely, if we dwell on evil thoughts, we will express those thoughts in evil actions. If we keep evil out of our thoughts, we will do the same in our actions.

Conflict negotiator Ken Sande noted that even if changing your focus to positive thoughts does not allow you to overlook the conflict, it can help you in two other important ways. "First, by recalling what is good in another person, you often will realize how much you will lose if your differences are not resolved. . . . Remembering the good may provide the motivation it takes to work through the painful differences that temporarily separate people. Second, the process of thinking right can be contagious. The more negatively you view your opponents, the more inclined they will be to view you in the same way. Conversely, as you focus on what is good about another person and openly acknowledge those qualities, he or she may begin to do the same in return" (*The Peacemaker,* 79).

Verse 9: **Those things, which ye have both learned, and received, and heard, and seen in me, do: and the God of peace shall be with you.**

Paul's fifth and final principle for developing an attitude that honors God during a conflict was practice what you've learned.

Paul used four verbs in this verse to describe what the Philippians knew of his own example. The first two verbs, **learned** and **received,** refer to Paul's instruction and teaching as he communicated Christian doctrine and Christian living to them. The next two verbs, **heard** and **seen,** refer to the Philippians' observation of Paul's life in both his speech and conduct. Paul had had to deal with intense conflict and opposition during his stay in Philippi (see Acts 16:16-40), so the believers had seen him in action.

Paul dared to tell his friends that they should practice what he did. **Do** renders *prasso,* "practice" (NIV). A present imperative form, it means they were to make it the habit of their lives. It was then that God's peace—and even more, **the God of peace**—would be with them. Christians who think and act in ways that please and honor God can be assured of His presence even in conflict situations.

Paul's instruction applied to the conflict between these two believers in ancient Philippi. His formula will apply equally well in your life in modern America.

July 12

ACCEPT RESPONSIBILITY

Background Scripture: Matthew 7:3-5; James 4:1-3,7-12
Focal Verses: Matthew 7:3-5; James 4:1-3,7-12

INTRODUCTION

1. As we learned from last week's lesson, "Honor God," peacemaking always begins by focusing on God and His concerns. *Glorify God* is the first of the four "G's" in resolving personal conflict.

2. Next, you need to focus on yourself and examine your attitudes and evaluate your faults and responsibilities in the conflict situation. This involves the second "G" in resolving personal conflict: *Get the Log out of Your Eye.*

3. When adults are in conflict situations, they often blame others. They tend to focus on the attitudes and behavior of others and to justify their own actions. Such responses usually prolong or escalate a conflict. What adults need to do instead is to ask themselves, "How do I accept responsibility for my part in a conflict situation?" When adults acknowledge and accept responsibility for the part they have had in a conflict, they open the door for resolution.

4. The Lesson Bible Truth is that in conflict situations, believers are to accept responsibility for their attitudes and actions that contribute to the conflict.

5. The Lesson Outcome is to help you accept responsibility for your part in conflict situations by confessing your wrongs and committing to change sinful attitudes and actions.

I. SOME PRELIMINARY CONSIDERATIONS

When you are ready to accept responsibility for your part in a conflict situation by confessing your wrongs and committing to change your sinful attitudes and actions, attorney Ken Sande of

Peacemaker Ministries, a Christian organization that seeks to equip and assist Christians to respond to conflict biblically, recommends *"The Seven A's of Confession."*

(1) *Address Everyone Involved.* You should confess your sins to every person who has been directly affected by your wrongdoings.

(2) *Avoid "If," "But," and "Maybe."* Don't try to excuse your wrongs by shifting the blame to others or minimizing or excusing your guilt.

(3) *Admit Specifically.* Specific admissions of your sinful attitudes and actions helps to convince others that you are honestly facing up to what you have done or to your part in the conflict situation.

(4) *Apologize.* Express sorrow for hurting someone. Apologizing shows the other person that you understand how he or she felt as a result of your words or actions.

(5) *Accept the Consequences.* Unless you are willing to do whatever you can to make restitution, the person you wronged may assume that you are simply trying to be released from your responsibilities. The harder you work to make restitution and repair the damage you caused, the easier it will be for others to believe your confession and be reconciled to you.

(6) *Alter Your Behavior.* Changing your attitudes and actions will help to demonstrate that your repentance is sincere.

(7) *Ask for Forgiveness and Allow Time.* This step moves the responsibility to the other person and allows that person to make and express a decision to forgive you.

(See Ken Sande, *The Peacemaker: A Biblical Guide to Resolving Personal Conflict*, 107-119.)

II. FOCAL VERSES EXAMINED
(Matt. 7:3-5; Jas. 4:1-3,7-12)

During His earthly ministry, Jesus had quite a bit to say about resolving conflict. In the Sermon on the Mount, Jesus told His disciples that before they confronted others about their faults they needed to face up to their own faults. Basically Jesus told them to evaluate themselves first. Only after you have dealt with your contribution to a conflict may you approach others about their part. James, our Lord's earthly brother, pointed to the inner source out of which conflicts arise and called his readers to submission and repentance.

1. Evaluate Yourself (Matt. 7:3-5)

Jesus instructed His disciples to remove the flaws, errors, and sins from their lives before they attempted to help others clean up their lives.

Verses 3-5: And why beholdest thou the mote [speck of dust] **that is in thy brother's eye, but considerest not the beam that is in thine own eye? ⁴Or how wilt thou say to thy brother, Let me pull out the mote out of thine eye; and, behold, a beam is in thine own eye? ⁵Thou hypocrite, first cast out the beam out of thine own eye; and then shalt thou see clearly to cast out the mote out of thy brother's eye.**

In these verses Jesus employed ironic humor to enable those guilty of criticizing other Christians to see themselves. In essence He said that we should use self-criticism before criticizing others, that we should use self-evaluation before we try to evaluate others.

A **mote** (*karphos*) is a speck, as dust, or a small chip or piece of straw. The *New International Version* translates it "speck of sawdust." A **beam** (*dokon*) is a large beam of wood or "plank" (NIV). Jesus envisioned a **hypocrite,** a *play actor,* with a large beam of wood in his own eye trying to remove a speck of dust from someone else's eye.

Jesus intended to picture the ridiculous. This picture, however, is no more ridiculous than for one Christian to set himself or herself up as the *watch dog* over another Christian's actions when his or her own faults or sins are even greater than the other believer's.

The words **beholdest** and **considerest** in verse 3 tell a picturesque story. One *looks at* the faults of another while ignoring much greater faults in one's own life—faults that render one unable to get close enough to the other believer to help him or her get rid of his or her sins.

What did Jesus say to do? **First cast out the beam out of thine own eye; and then shalt thou see clearly to cast out the mote out of thy brother's eye.** We first should see that our own lives are within the Lord's will. Then in Christian love we should render aid to those brothers and sisters who are less so. This is seen in the Greek words for **beholdest** (v. 3) and **see clearly** (v. 5). The former is *blepeis*, which simply means "to look at" or "to see" someone or something. The latter is *diablepseis,* which means "to look through" (*dia,* "through," plus *blepeis,* "to look at" or "to see") a thing. The carping critic simply *sees* another person's faults, but a sympathetic Christian *sees through* another in order to comprehend the situation. "Seeing through" (*diablepseis*) will produce a bond of sympathy between the two. Then the stronger will be able to help the weaker to correct his or her faults and to avoid other faults.

In a conflict, before we blame or criticize others, as Christians we are to evaluate ourselves and accept responsibility for our part in the conflict.

2. Recognize Conflict's Source (Jas. 4:1-3)

Sinful desires cause conflicts between believers and affect their relationships with God.

Verse 1: **From whence come wars and fightings among you? come they not hence, even of your lusts that war in your members?**

Wars and fightings usually refer to conflicts between nations. In this context, however, they refer to conflict situations within the church fellowship. In the Greek text the word for **whence** (*pothen*) is used with both **wars** and **fightings.** This shows how intensely James was concerned about the situation. **Wars** pictures the chronic state of rivalry which on occasion erupted into a battle between factions.

A. T. Robertson (*Word Pictures in the New Testament,* vol. 6, 49) wrote, "The origin of a war or of any quarrel is sometimes hard to find, but James touches the sore spot here." Whence, indeed, do such things come? They come "out of" (*ek*, indicating the source) **your lusts that war in your members. Lusts** translates *hedonon*, which means "pleasures." Our word *hedonism* comes from this Greek word. *Hedonism* is desiring pleasure, enjoyment, recognition, or self-gratification. Instead of expressing selfless love (*agape*) toward others, hedonism is living selfishly. *Hedone* is translated variously: "passions" (RSV), "pleasures" (NASB), "cravings" (NRSV), "cravings for pleasure" (Beck), "desires" (NIV, Williams), "desires for pleasures" (Phillips), "selfish desires" (CEV), "the appetites" (REB). The word is found only in three other places in the New Testament (Luke 8:14; Titus 3:3; 2 Pet. 2:13) and always is used in a bad sense. It pictures lives that are self-centered, not God-centered or other-centered. It means to have one's way or to please oneself, regardless of the best interests of others.

The word for **war** in verse 1b is *strateuo*, "to carry on a military campaign." This hedonistic war is **in,** or "in the sphere of" (*en*), **your members. The your in your members** is plural (*humon*). **Members** is vague. James may have been referring to parts of the human body, including the mind; or he may have been referring to church members, that is, to members of the community of faith. Does **in your members** refer to "within you" (as NIV) or to "in your midst"? Was James referring to inner personal struggles (as in 1:13-15), or was he referring to conflict and fighting within the life of the church (as vv. 2-10 seem to indicate)? Either way, such conflict should be foreign to Christians. So the figure is that of a foreign army who has invaded the Christian fellowship (or the believer) and has carried out its campaigns among the believers (or within the believer).

Verse 2a: **Ye lust, and have not: ye kill, and desire to have, and cannot obtain: ye fight and war.**

Verse 2 has a punctuation problem. Various translations have attempted to make the meaning of this verse clearer by changing its punctuation. The original Greek manuscripts had no punctuation except the question mark. Thus the punctuation is not inspired. It may read: **Ye lust, and have not.** [Therefore] **ye**

kill. And desire to have, and cannot obtain. [Therefore] **ye fight and war.** Or, like the *New International Version,* it may read: "You want something but don't get it. You kill and covet, but you cannot have what you want. You quarrel and fight."

Lust renders the word for desire (*epithumeo*). This word may be used in either a good or a bad sense. God has given us legitimate desires, such as the acquisitive instinct or the instinct that enables us to acquire things. Satan seeks to pervert our desire into *lust,* which causes us to acquire what we desire in an illegitimate way. So we lust after something—wealth, power, recognition, fame, or whatever. And when we do not obtain it, we are ready to **kill** for it.

In this context, we are not bound to see physical murder in **kill.** The Greek word is used for murder, but here the present indicative form means to do so repeatedly or habitually. If James was referring to physical murder, he indicated a bloody carnage within the church fellowship. No. James had a remarkable familiarity with the Sermon on the Mount. In Matthew 5:21 Jesus used the same verb for **kill** as James did here. Jesus showed that the source of the overt act is in one's attitude— anger and contempt—toward a person. Apparently this is the sense in which James used the word **kill.** Whatever it was for which the readers lusted, they sought to obtain it regardless of their attitude toward others or the rights of others.

Desire is a different word than that translated **lust.** In this context, the word translated **lust** expresses a strong, evil desire. **Desire** is the word *zeloute.* In the good sense, it means "to burn with zeal," "zealous." In the bad sense, as here, it means to "crave" (TCNT), to be "envious" (NASB, REB), or to be "jealous" (NCV) for something belonging to another. It means to "covet" (NIV, NRSV). Thus it is forbidden by the Tenth Commandment (Ex. 20:17). Failure to obtain the object of covetous desire produced fighting and war within the fellowship.

The object of evil desire may or may not be a material thing, such as money or property. It may be another person's beauty, influence, position, or talent. But whatever it is, the same evil desires are still the source of strife among many Christians.

Verses 2b-3: **Yet ye have not, because ye ask not. ³Ye ask, and receive not, because ye ask amiss, that ye may consume it upon your lusts.**

James told why his readers did not have what they so eagerly and evilly desired. It was because of a lack of prayer—**ye ask not** refers to requests to God. This assumed, of course, that the thing desired was good within itself when used properly. Instead of lusting for something that results in conflict, we should make it a matter of prayer—assuming, of course, that it is something about which one should pray.

Perhaps some had done so—**ye ask**—without receiving that for which they prayed—**and receive not.** James gave two reasons for this, reasons that in reality were one: (1) **Ye ask amiss.** **Amiss** (*kakos*) means "evilly" or "with evil intent." The *New International Version* and the *New American Standard Bible* read, "You ask with wrong motives." **Ask** here is an indirect middle (reflexive) form. "Ye ask for yourselves" or for selfish gratification. They did not ask God for what they wanted with the purpose of being better able to serve Him or their fellow believers. The request was wholly selfish and apart from God's will and purpose. It was the attitude of, "I want it because I want it!" (2) They prayed for things. James wrote, **Ye ask amiss, that ye may consume it upon your lusts.** The Greek word for **consume** (*dapanan*) means "squander" (REB) or "spend" (NIV). It refers to indulging in "wasteful spending." The word translated **lusts** is *hedonais* (see v. 1), "your pleasures" (NIV). In the Greek text **your lusts** is emphatic. It was not for the purpose of serving the Lord but for selfish pleasure that they asked—and God does not grant such prayers.

As Christians, when we are in a conflict situation, we need to admit our sinful actions and to face up to our sinful desires and attitudes—for these are the root cause of most conflicts.

3. Submit to God's Judgment (Jas. 4:7-12)

Using ten imperatives in four verses (vv. 7-10), James called his readers to submission and repentance. He warned that

Christians who speak evil against others set themselves up as judges and assume a position that belongs only to God. All ten imperatives are in the aorist tense. The aorist tense calls for immediate action, and the imperative mood expresses a command that adds a note of urgency to the verb tenses.

Verses 7-10: **Submit yourselves therefore to God. Resist the devil, and he will flee from you. [8]Draw nigh to God, and he will draw nigh to you. Cleanse your hands, ye sinners; and purify your hearts, ye double-minded. [9]Be afflicted, and mourn, and weep: let your laughter be turned to mourning, and your joy to heaviness. [10]Humble yourselves in the sight of the Lord, and he shall lift you up.**

First, **submit yourselves . . . to God. Submit** or "be subject to" is a verb that means "to be lined up as troops in orderly fashion under their commander." This denotes that we are God's troops, that we are under His command, and that we are to be obedient to His will. Instead of God fighting against us, we are to be on His side fighting for Him. When we take this position, it means that we have all His power at our disposal.

Second, **resist the devil.** In contrast to submitting to God, we are to "stand over against" or "take a stand against" (*antistete*; *anti,* "against," *histemi,* "to stand"; see Eph. 6:13; 1 Pet. 5:7) the **devil.** Lined up as troops under God's command, we are to stand in battle array against the devil.

These two commands go together. If you resist the devil in your own power alone, he will win every time. But if you submit yourself to God and are equipped with His power, and then resist the devil, **he will flee from you.** In God's strength, you must "stand up to the devil, and he will turn and run" (REB). Submission to God results in resistance to the devil. You cannot be submissive to God and neutral toward the devil anymore than a loyal soldier can be neutral toward his country's enemy in war.

Third, **draw nigh to God.** James said that submission to God involves not only resistance to the devil but drawing near to God with the assurance that **he will draw nigh to you.** In our struggle against temptation, we are not alone. As the battle rages and we are hard pressed, it is both encouraging and strengthening to know that our Commander fights with and for us—standing by our side as we face the foe.

Furthermore, this allegiance calls for purity of life. The fourth and fifth imperatives show that this purity is expressed outwardly by **cleanse your hands** and inwardly by **purify your hearts.** The psalmist asked and answered a question: "Who shall ascend into the hill of the Lord? or who shall stand in his holy place? He that hath clean hands and a pure heart" (Ps. 24:3-4). James may have had these words in mind about entering God's presence in the Jewish temple as he applied them to Christians enjoying God's presence.

James called his readers **sinners** and **double-minded,** or literally, "double-souled" (*dipsychoi*). The word **sinners** refers to those who have missed the mark of God's character and will. **Double-minded** describes those who try to hold on to both God and the world. James urged them to forsake the world and give undivided loyalty to God (see Matt. 6:24).

Three more imperatives—the sixth, seventh, and eighth— describe a deeply repentant state of heart and mind—**be afflicted, and mourn, and weep. Afflicted** means to endure toils. It suggests bearing the burden of conviction and guilt. **Mourn** means to mourn as for the dead, so it refers to deep mourning over one's sins. **Weep** denotes the outward expression of inward grief.

James did not forbid **laughter** and **joy** as such when he wrote in his ninth imperative to **let your laughter be turned to mourning, and your joy to heaviness.** In their proper setting both are God's wonderful gifts to us. But the setting here was one that should call for sorrow. James used these terms in the sense of "hilarity and merry-making" (Curtis Vaughan, *James: A Study Guide Commentary* [Grand Rapids: Zondervan Publishing House, 1969], 92) when the situation called for deep sadness and concern. We should not make light of our sins. Instead, our sins should produce **mourning** and **heaviness. Heaviness** (*katepseia*) appears only here in the Bible. It connotes "gloom" (NIV), dejection, or depression that often is due to shame.

The tenth imperative is **humble yourselves in the sight of the Lord.** In humbling ourselves before God we recognize His great glory and right to rule in our lives. By comparison, it shows our own insignificance and unworthiness of His grace and love. When we humble ourselves **in the sight of the Lord,** James wrote, **he** [God] **shall lift you up.**

Verses 11-12: **Speak not evil one of another, brethren. He that speaketh evil of his brother, and judgeth his brother, speaketh evil of the law, and judgeth the law: but if thou judge the law, thou art not a doer of the law, but a judge.** [12]**There is one lawgiver, who is able to save and to destroy: who art thou that judgest another?**

In verses 1-10 James dealt with sins related to lust for pleasure and self-gratification. But there is still another type of sin that mars our Christian lives and disturbs the church fellowship—criticism of others. This sin is expressed through the wrong use of the tongue. Someone has described the tongue as the only tool that grows sharper by constant use. This is never more evident than in gossip, undue criticism of others, and verbal conflict.

Verse 11 begins with another imperative, but this time it is a present tense—**Speak not.** The present imperative form indicates either "stop doing it" or "do not have the habit of doing it." In this context the former sense seems preferable.

Evil is not in the Greek text. The sense is derived from the meaning of the verb **speak.** James used the verb *katalaleo,* a compound verb comprised of *kata,* "against" or "down," and *lalein,* "to speak" or "to talk." Robertson (*Word Pictures in the New Testament,* vol. 6, 54) said that it often means to speak harsh words about someone who is not present. The word could refer to gossip, harsh criticism, or speaking disparagingly of someone—running someone down with an irresponsible tongue. The *New International Version* reads "slander."

The one who speaks against **his brother . . . judgeth his brother.** Notice James's repeated use of **brother** and **brethren** to emphasize the evil nature of the act. Furthermore, to speak evil against a fellow believer is to show one's contempt for and judgment of God's law—he **speaketh evil of the law, and judgeth the law.**

Did James have in mind any particular law of God? When seen in regard to attitude, it could include such Commandments as those forbidding murder, theft (of one's good name), or bearing false witness. Indeed, as James showed, it could even refer to the First Commandment because the critic sets himself up in place of God—**there is one lawgiver.** Perhaps we can best understand this law as the "royal law" of James 2:8: "Thou shalt love thy neighbor as thyself." This law summarizes the Commandments dealing with our relationships to other people.

In setting yourself up as your brother's judge, you actually become a self-appointed judge of God's law. In so doing you say, in effect, that God's law is not worthy of your obedience. Thus instead of being a **doer** of God's law, you become its **judge.** You usurp God's place and authority. Since God is the only **lawgiver**—and following different manuscript traditions the *New International Version* adds "and Judge"—He alone has the power **to save and to destroy.** He is Lord of both life and death. There is also here an anticipation of the final judgment. God gave His law, and He alone is the competent Judge of those who violate it—including those who judge their fellow believers.

In conflict situations many people tend to rationalize their actions and judge themselves by their own standards or by society's standards. As Christians, we are to submit ourselves to God and to His standard in Scripture when we are evaluating our part in a conflict.

Accept responsibility for your own attitudes and actions. Stop blaming others. Stop trying to justify your behaviors that have contributed to a conflict. Deal with yourself before you try to deal with someone else. Get the log out of your own eye!

July 19

CONFRONT IN LOVE

Background Scripture: Matthew 18:15-17;
Galatians 5:13–6:5
Focal Verses: Matthew 18:15-17; Galatians 5:13-15; 6:1-5

INTRODUCTION

1. Once you have identified God's concerns and taken responsibility for your contribution to a conflict, it may be necessary to talk to others about *their* shortcomings.

2. Many people who are involved in conflict do not like to confront the other party. This often allows bitterness to grow and prevents a proper solution. Other people confront too quickly and harshly, which usually makes conflict worse. When people who are in conflict confront each other in love, they are more likely to avoid adversarial situations and to find constructive solutions to their problems.

3. But you may ask yourself, *How can I confront someone in a loving manner that will help resolve a conflict?*

4. The Lesson Bible Truth is that when confrontation is necessary to resolve conflict, Christians are to confront in love in order to restore relationships.

5. The Lesson Outcome is to help you be equipped to confront others in a loving manner when involved in conflict situations.

I. SOME PRELIMINARY CONSIDERATIONS

The Third "G"

In this study theme we have been identifying, explaining, and illustrating four essentials of peacemaking that are revealed in God's Word. These principles center in four "G's." We already have looked at the first two: "*G*lorify God" and "*G*et the Log Out of Your Eye." In this lesson we turn to the third—"*G*o and Show

66

Your Brother His Fault." This lesson deals with attempting to resolve conflict by confronting other believers in love.

II. FOCAL VERSES EXAMINED
(Matt. 18:15-17; Gal. 5:13-15; 6:1-5)

In Matthew 18:15-17 Jesus detailed a fourfold *process* for attempting to resolve a conflict situation between two believers. When Paul wrote to the Galatians, he wrote to a church in conflict. In chapter 5 he offered an important *principle* about serving others in love. In chapter 6 he examined the *purpose* of confronting other believers in love.

1. Process (Matt. 18:15-17)

Believers are to follow biblical guidelines in seeking to resolve conflict. Jesus detailed a fourfold process for attempting to resolve a conflict situation between two believers. First, the offended party is to go to the offender and seek to straighten out the matter between them. Second, if this attempt is rebuffed, the offended party is to take one or two others along in the attempt at resolution. If this attempt to resolve the issue also is rebuffed, then the third step is for the church to become involved in seeking to settle the dispute. Finally, if the offender persists in his or her belligerence, the church is to treat the rebellious offender as an unbeliever. Such action is designed to correct and strengthen an offending believer.

Verse 15: **Moreover if thy brother shall trespass against thee, go and tell him his fault between thee and him alone: if he shall hear thee, thou hast gained thy brother.**

The two uses of **brother** assume a matter between two believers. The word **trespass** (*hamartese*) translates the verb for "sins" (NIV). In a conflict situation, should the one who was wronged wait until the wrongdoer comes to him? No. Jesus told the wronged party to take the first step. The one who was wronged is to **go** to the wrongdoer **and tell him his fault.** When the person who was wronged takes this action, it is to be

between thee and him alone—or "just between the two of you" (NIV). So often the case is the opposite. The wronged party tells everybody but the wrongdoer. When this is done, the person who was wronged becomes a wrongdoer too. Thus the breach is widened, not healed. If the offending believer listens to you and responds positively, **thou hast gained,** or "reclaimed," **thy brother.**

Since this first step of talking privately with your opponent is vitally important, Ken Sande, executive director of Peacemaker Ministries, suggested several ingredients about biblical confrontation. Among these are: choose the right time and place, plan your words, speak to build up the other person, use "I" statements since these give information about yourself rather than attack the other person, offer possible solutions, ask for feedback, be quick to listen, and recognize your limits (*The Peacemaker,* 146-167). Remember, in such meetings "your purpose should be to *win others over* not to win over them" (Sande, *The Peacemaker,* 170).

Verse 16: **But if he will not hear thee, then take with thee one or two more, that in the mouth of two or three witnesses every word may be established.**

Having given the first step to be taken, Jesus then stated the second. He assumed that the first step might fail. Failure in the first does not free the wronged party from further effort to resolve the conflict. But the person who was wronged is not to try again alone.

The second step involves the wronged person taking **one or two more** persons who are uninvolved in the conflict with him. This procedure is based on Deuteronomy 19:15: "At the mouth of two witnesses, or at the mouth of three witnesses, shall the matter be established." The wronged party plus one would be two witnesses; another would provide three witnesses. Perhaps and preferably these individuals would be agreeable to both parties—mutual friends, neutral individuals, or respected church leaders. Such conciliators may facilitate communication, help determine the facts, ask appropriate questions, give advice on how to deal with the problem, offer practical solutions based on their own experience, help resolve a deadlock, serve as arbitrators, encourage reconciliation by pleading with the wrongdoer, or—if the wrongdoer refuses to listen—serve as witnesses who later report what they observed during the conciliation efforts.

The quotation from Deuteronomy 19:15 refers to **every word** (*pan rhema*) being **established.** On this matter, Ken Sande noted that "words play a key role in almost every conflict. When words are used properly, words promote understanding and encourage agreement. When misused, they usually aggravate offenses and drive people further apart" (*The Peacemaker,* 146). In conflict situations it is especially important to watch how you use your words.

Verse 17a: **And if he shall neglect to hear them, tell it unto the church.**

Then Jesus gave the third step. Failing in the first two attempts, the matter is to be brought before the local church. **Tell it unto the church** does not mean that one is to stand up during a worship service and broadcast the details of the conflict to the whole church and to anyone else who happens to be visiting that Sunday! Rather, this instruction shows that the local church has the right and responsibility to arbitrate such matters in an attempt to end the conflict and restore the broken relationships. The instruction probably relates to informing the church leadership and requesting their assistance in resolving the matter.

Verse 17b: **But if he neglect to hear the church, let him be unto thee as an heathen man and a publican.**

The fourth step is the most drastic. If the wrongdoer refuses to listen to the church, he is to be treated as a **heathen man and a publican. Heathen** (*ethnikos*) literally is "Gentile" or "pagan" (NIV). A **publican** (*telones*) is a "tax collector" (NIV). For Jews, both of these were social outcasts.

What is involved in this? Jesus' procedure may mean that by his actions the wrongdoer shows he is not a believer. If so, the church simply accepts that fact, which means that he never really was a part of the fellowship of believers. But since Jesus spoke of him as **thy brother** in verse 15, the implication is that he is a believer. Further, Jesus did not say he was a pagan; He said, **Let him be unto thee *as* an heathen man** (emphasis added). Jesus' use of the word **as** (*hosper*) is significant. Only God can know whether a person truly is a believer. But if one who claims to be a believer behaves like a nonbeliever, the church is to treat him or her *as* a nonbeliever. The church takes this action to recognize that he or she is out of fellowship by his or her own choice. The church's action recognizes a condition that the transgressor has created and maintains. At the same time, this action does not mean that the church is not willing to receive back into its fellowship one who is willing to be received as a brother after a change in attitude and conduct on the part of the wrongdoer.

Such is Jesus' fourfold process for resolving a conflict situation that believers are to follow.

2. Principle (Gal. 5:13-15)

Throughout his epistle to the Galatian believers, Paul championed spiritual freedom for Gentile Christians against the legalism of the Judaizers. But apparently he found himself faced with another problem—conflict within the fellowship. This conflict posed an even greater immediate threat to the churches than that of the Judaizers' false teachings, so Paul laid down an important principle—the principle of love.

Verses 13-14: **For, brethren, ye have been called unto liberty; only use not liberty for an occasion to the flesh, but by love serve one another. [14]For all the law is fulfilled in one word, even in this; Thou shalt love thy neighbor as thyself.**

Paul warned the Galatians not to use their **liberty** in Christ as an **occasion to the flesh. Flesh** (*sarki*) is used to refer to the fallen, corrupted, sinful nature—not to the physical body. The *New International Version* brings out this ethical sense better by translating the word "sinful nature." **Occasion** (*aphormen*) renders a word that originally denoted a military base from which an attack could be launched. Paul was fond of using military terms, and (except for Luke 11:54 in some manuscripts) he alone used this word in the New Testament (see Rom. 7:8,11; 2 Cor. 5:12; 11:12; 1 Tim. 5:14). Believers are not to use their freedom "as a pretext" or "as an opportunity" or "as an occasion" for actions that are contrary to their spiritual position in Christ.

The Christian alternative to such is **by love** [to] **serve one another.** Love (*agape*) connotes unselfish love toward one another. In this God-type-of-love, believers literally are to "serve as slaves" (*douleuete*) to each other. Why? Because every single part of the **law—all the law**—or the Ten Commandments is fulfilled **in one word.** That is, "The entire law is summed up in a single command" (NIV). The Jewish rabbis combined Deuteronomy 6:5, about loving God, and Leviticus 19:18, about loving one's neighbor, to create a summary of the two tablets of the law (see Matt. 22:37-40). Paul cited only the latter—**Thou shalt love thy neighbor as thyself**—since the current problem centered around relationships in conflict. When there are disagreements and conflicts, they should be swallowed up in the greater principle of love.

"We are not released from the command to love our neighbor as ourselves even when that neighbor is hating, cursing, and mistreating us" (Sande, *The Peacemaker,* 28). Conflict provides another opportunity to "serve as slaves" others.

Verse 15: But if ye bite and devour one another, take heed that ye be not consumed one of another.

In this verse Paul came to the crux of the matter. The construction of the conditional sentence, **if ye,** is a first-class condition in the Greek. It assumes the reality of the situation described. **Bite and devour** describe wild animals fighting among themselves. The words are present tense—"if you keep on biting" and "if you keep on tearing to pieces." Such vicious *selfishness* is far from the ideal *selflessness* of Christian love. Certainly Christ did not set believers free for such!

Take heed may read better as "beware" or "watch out" (NIV). If such conflict continued, the churches and believers of Galatia would **be . . . consumed,** "annihilated," or "destroyed" (NIV) by themselves.

And so the principle is that, as Christians, we are responsible to act in love toward others even in conflict situations. When we do so, we serve the other person and help keep the conflict from getting worse.

3. Purpose (Gal. 6:1-5)

Why should believers lovingly confront others with whom they have conflicts? What is the purpose of doing so? The purpose of loving confrontation is to restore fellow believers to spiritual health.

Verse 1: **Brethren, if a man be overtaken in a fault, ye which are spiritual, restore such an one in the spirit of meekness; considering thyself, lest thou also be tempted.**

Paul pictured a problem situation. We might call this a *prolambano* situation. Paul's construction of the conditional clause **if a man be overtaken in a fault** is a future more probable condition. This Greek grammatical construction, known as a third class condition, suggests the probability of such a situation in the future. **Man** (*anthropos*) is used generically. Some early manuscripts make this clear by reading "if anyone" or "if someone" (the indefinite pronoun), hence the *New International Version*'s "if someone." **Overtaken** (*prolemphthe,* a third person singular aorist subjunctive passive from *prolambano*) renders a verb meaning to be "taken by surprise," "seized unaware," "overtaken," "entrapped" or "caught" (NIV). The word for **fault** (*paraptomati*) or "sin" (NIV) literally means "fall aside," "slip," "make a false step," or "lapse." In the New Testament the word is used repeatedly in the ethical sense. It could apply to any moral slip.

One might picture the situation Paul described as a fisherman who wasn't paying attention and became entangled in his net as it was going overboard and he was now in danger of drowning. Both the fisherman and the believer caught in sin have the same need—their problems have become so serious that they are not able to save themselves. They need someone else to step in and cut the cords that entangle them. Just as you would not stand by and watch a fisherman drown while entangled in his net, neither should you stand by and watch another believer be destroyed by his sin. If sin appears to be dragging your brother or sister in Christ under, it is your responsibility to try to help him or her.

But what should you do in such a problematic situation? In presenting the proper course of action, Paul showed in verse 1 *what* to do, *who* should do it, and *how* it should be done (James Montgomery Boice, "Galatians," in *The Expositor's Bible Commentary,* vol. 10 [Grand Rapids: Zondervan Publishing House, 1976], 501).

Paul instructed the believers *what* they should do. We might call this the *katartizo* principle. They should **restore** their fellow believer who is entrapped in sin. **Restore** (*katartizete*) translates an imperative verb that was used in the commercial sphere of mending or repairing fishing nets (see Matt. 4:21; Mark 1:19). In secular Greek it was used in the medical arena of setting broken bones so that they would be strong again. It was used in religious contexts of completing or perfecting one's faith (see 2 Cor. 13:11; 1 Thess. 3:10; Heb. 13:21). And it was used in ethical contexts of restoring one to a former good state (see 1 Cor. 1:10). All of these meanings make sense here: mend what is torn; set straight that which is fractured; equip one to overcome the problem; and restore one to a right moral condition. "Each of these activities has the goal of making something or someone useful for its intended purpose" (Ken Sande, *The Peacemaker,* 140). These figures also suggest person-to-person relationships. They further suggest the need for patience, skill, and persistent effort by the one doing them until the completion of the task. "What is wrong in the life of a fallen Christian is to be set straight. It is not to be neglected or exposed openly" (Boice, "Galatians," 501). Damaged or broken believers whose sins have hurt their spiritual health and reduced their usefulness to God need to be and are to be mended and restored to usefulness in God's kingdom.

Next, Paul instructed the believers about *who* should do the work of restoring. He said it was those who are **spiritual** (*pneumatikoi*). "Only those who are genuinely led of the Spirit have the maturity to deal with sin in others" (Boice, "Galatians," 501).

Third, Paul told *how* it should be done. The restoration should be made **in the spirit of meekness.** Meekness (*prautetos*) is the same word used in 5:23 for the fruit of the Spirit. A better translation is "gentleness" (NASB, NRSV) or "gently" (NIV). It is the opposite of an arrogant and self-assertive spirit. This attempt to restore a believer entrapped by sin should also be done with the consciousness that no one has immunity from temptation. We all are vulnerable to moral failings. Hence Paul's warning to "look at," "take notice of," "watch," or "take heed" (*skopon*) about yourself—**considering thyself.** This is to be done **lest thou also be tempted** (*peirasthes*) or "solicited to sin."

Verse 2: Bear ye one another's burdens, and so fulfill the law of Christ.

One another's occurs first in the sentence, and so is emphatic. The noun rendered **burdens** (*bare*) literally means "weight," but it is used in the New Testament to refer to oppressive burdens or crushing loads too heavy to be borne alone (Matt. 20:12; Acts 15:28; 1 Thess. 2:7; Rev. 2:24). A load that would crush one person alone can be successfully borne by two or more. So the one who is heavy-laden or burdened with temptation will be strengthened to find that help from others is at hand. "In this manner" (*houtos*), Paul wrote, "you will fulfill" (future tense) **the law of Christ.** What is **the law of Christ?** It is the command to love that was given in 5:13b-14. John Fawcett (1740-1817) caught the sense of what Paul was saying:

> We share our mutual woes,
> Our mutual burdens bear;
> And often for each other flows
> The sympathizing tear.

("Blest Be the Tie," No. 387, *The Baptist Hymnal,* 1991.)

Two errors might keep a believer from exercising the law of love in relation to fellow believers. Paul addressed one of these errors in verse 3, and he addressed the second error in verse 4. The first error is conceit.

Verse 3: **For if a man think himself to be something, when he is nothing, he deceiveth himself.**

To be conceited is to think yourself more important than you are. If you think you're above helping another believer bear a heavy burden, that shows you're really **nothing** (*meden*)—a real *zero*—rather than **something** (*tis*). It also shows that you're self-deceived. This is the only time the verb translated **deceiveth** (*phrenapata*) appears in the New Testament—or in any Greek literature, except Christian writings after Paul. Paul probably coined the term himself from the word for "mind" (*phren*) and the verb for "delusion" and "deceit" (*apate*). In other words, Paul said, "You've deluded your own minds; you're your own mind-misleader."

Verse 4: **But let every man prove his own work, and then shall he have rejoicing in himself alone, and not in another.**

The second error that might prevent believers from practicing Christ's law of love is to be always comparing themselves and their **own work** with others. Paul reminded the believers that before they confront others in love, they need to reexamine their own actions and attitudes by the same standards they apply to others. **Prove** means "to examine" or "to test" (NIV) something, as is done with metals, to see if it is genuine or false. If one finds his own work genuine, **then shall he have rejoicing** that by God's grace he is as he is. The word **rejoicing** (*kauchema*) carries the idea of exultation or congratulation, but it is limited by and restricted to **in himself** (*eis heauton*) and **alone** (*monon*). He is not to parade his goodness before **another. Another** renders *heteron*, "another of a different kind," that is, before a weak believer as opposed to a mature believer.

In other words, "the rationale for testing one's own actions is so that 'then' such a one 'will have a basis for boasting in himself, and not by comparison with someone else.' The warning here is not to live as spiritual people in a state of pride or conceit, always comparing one's own attainments to those of others and so feeling superior, but rather to test one's own actions and so to minimize the possibility of self-deception. Christian feelings of exultation and congratulation should spring from one's own actions as seen in the light of God's approval and not derive from comparing oneself to what others are or are not doing" (Richard N. Longenecker, "Galatians," in the *Word Biblical Commentary,* vol. 41 [Dallas: Word Books, Publishers, 1990], 277).

Verse 5: For every man shall bear his own burden.

There is no contradiction between this verse and verse 2, as it may appear from the *King James Version.* The word used here for **burden** (*phortion*) is a different word from that used in verse 2 (*bare*). And even though these words sometimes were used interchangeably, Paul obviously used them to draw a contrast between crushing burdens (v. 2) and those burdens that a person can bear alone (v. 5). (See Herschel H. Hobbs, *Galatians: A Verse By Verse Study* [Waco: Word Books, Publishers, 1978], 139-140 versus Richard Longenecker, "Galatians," 277-278). This is the word Jesus used when He spoke of His burden being light (Matt. 11:30). It is the common term for a soldier's "pack." J. B. Phillips caught this sense nicely in his translation: "For every man must 'shoulder his own pack.'" **Every man** is again generic—"each one" (NIV, NASB) or "everyone" (*hekastos*). In other words, we should not impose on others in areas where we can help ourselves.

A famous ancient rabbi once reflected, "I wonder whether there is anyone in these times who accepts reproof." Another rabbi responded, "I wonder whether there is anyone in these times who knows how to give admonition." Yes, dear brothers and sisters, it may be necessary to confront others about their faults and shortcomings in attempting to resolve a conflict situation and to restore relationships; but we always must confront others in love—this is the law of Christ.

July 26

BE RECONCILED

Background Scripture: Genesis 50:15-21;
                Matthew 5:21-26; Colossians 3:12-17
Focal Verses: Genesis 50:15-21; Matthew 5:23-24;
            Colossians 3:12-15

INTRODUCTION

1. Many adults never attempt to be reconciled to people with whom they have had a conflict or with whom they presently are having a conflict.

2. Others have an inadequate concept of reconciliation. They say they have forgiven someone who has wronged them, but they continue to think about the incident or talk about it with others. They also may use the incident against the person, or they may allow the incident to stand between them and hinder their relationship.

3. And so you may wonder, *How do I pursue genuine reconciliation in a conflict situation?*

4. The Lesson Bible Truth is that Christians are to take the necessary actions to be reconciled to others in a conflict situation.

5. The Lesson Outcome is to help you pursue genuine reconciliation in conflict situations.

I. SOME PRELIMINARY CONSIDERATIONS

1. The Fourth "G"

We now come to the conclusion of this study theme in which we have been identifying, explaining, and illustrating four essentials of peacemaking that are revealed in God's Word. Each of the four principles begins with a "G": "*G*lorify God," "*G*et the Log Out of Your Eye," "*G*o and Show Your Brother His Fault," and "*G*o and Be Reconciled."

2. Reconciliation and the End of Conflict

Reconciliation is the final step in resolving a conflict. To be reconciled means that peace, friendship, and fellowship have replaced hostility, opposition, and separation. Before complete reconciliation can occur, the personal offenses that separated opponents must be laid to rest through confession and forgiveness. This is why believers must be ready to restore relationships, make reconciliation a priority, and forgive completely.

II. FOCAL VERSES EXAMINED
(Gen. 50:15-21; Matt. 5:23-24; Col. 3:12-15)

In the story of Joseph's dealing with his brothers after their father Jacob's death, we see an example of one who was willing and ready to restore broken relationships. From Jesus' words in the Sermon on the Mount, we learn that reconciliation with a fellow believer is to be a top priority, even more than worshiping God or giving gifts to Him. Paul's admonitions to the Colossians show us that we are to forgive completely and provide the occasion for us to discuss how we can do it.

1. Be Ready to Restore Relationships (Gen. 50:15-21)

Joseph was the firstborn son of Rachel, Jacob's beloved. The fact that Joseph entertained visions of grandeur led his ten older brothers to hate him. Eventually they caused Joseph to be sold into slavery in Egypt. Joseph's first two experiences in the new land were disasters for him. But eventually, by interpreting Pharaoh's dreams, he was elevated to the second place of power in Egypt. His primary task was, during seven years of plenty, to store up grain against seven lean years.

The widespread famine brought Joseph's ten brothers to Egypt to buy grain. Joseph recognized them, but they did not recognize him. Finally, after a series of incidents in which Joseph tested their character and attitude, he revealed his identity to them. After that, Jacob and his family moved to Egypt.

They lived in the land of Goshen, the most fertile area in the land. Before Jacob died, he blessed his twelve sons and the sons of Joseph. The closing chapter of Genesis tells of Jacob's death after a sojourn of 17 years in Egypt (see Gen. 47:28). When Jacob's sons returned from burying him in Hebron, the place where Abraham and Isaac were buried, the ten brothers wondered about their own safety now that their father was dead.

Verse 15: **And when Joseph's brethren saw that their father was dead, they said, Joseph will peradventure hate us, and will certainly requite us all the evil which we did unto him.**

Evidently they read into Joseph their own attitude. If he had been a vengeful person, he was certainly in a position to vent his hatred on them. They apparently felt that his love for them was not genuine but was faked for Jacob's sake. Now that their father was dead, would Joseph show his true nature to be one who wanted to get even with them for what they had done to him? No. Jacob's true nature was one of forgiveness.

Verses 16-18: **And they sent a messenger unto Joseph, saying, Thy father did command before he died, saying, ¹⁷So shall ye say unto Joseph, Forgive, I pray thee now, the trespass of thy brethren, and their sin; for they did unto thee evil: and now, we pray thee, forgive the trespass of the servants of the God of thy father. And Joseph wept when they spake unto him. ¹⁸And his brethren also went and fell down before his face; and they said, Behold, we be thy servants.**

At one time Joseph was at the mercy of his brothers and received none—except that instead of killing him they sold him into slavery. But now they were at his mercy—and they received it.

At first the brothers **sent a messenger** or a deputation to plead their case. The plea was based on a dying **command** of their father that Joseph should **forgive** them. No such command is recorded in the Bible. Nor is Jacob recorded as giving such a command to Joseph, even though Joseph was with his father when he died (Gen. 49:33–50:1). More likely, this was a story manufactured by the brothers, a story that shows their guilt.

On hearing this plea, Joseph **wept.** Eventually the brothers came to Joseph. Perhaps the report of his tears led them to believe that he meant them no harm. In typical oriental fashion they **fell down** on their faces before him, declaring themselves to be his **servants.** Joseph's dreams had become a reality (see Gen. 37:5-10). But the passing of time and the experiences through which he had gone had made Joseph a different person than he was as a lad of 17.

Verses 19-20: **And Joseph said unto them, Fear not: for am I in the place of God? 20But as for you, ye thought evil against me; but God meant it unto good, to bring to pass, as it is this day, to save much people alive. 21Now therefore fear ye not: I will nourish you, and your little ones. And he comforted them, and spake kindly unto them.**

Joseph's question about his not being God apparently referred to his brothers' fear of punishment at the hands of their brother. They had no need to **fear** him; he had forgiven them. If they were to be judged, that was God's prerogative. Joseph acknowledged his brothers' evil intent toward him—**ye thought evil against me**—but he had come to see that God had overruled the evil in order to bring **good** out of the situation.

In reassuring his brothers that they had no need to fear him, Joseph did three things. First, he promised them, **I will nourish you, and your little ones.** This means that he would provide for them and their children. Second, **he comforted them.** And third, he **spake kindly unto them.**

Joseph took this attitude toward those who had wronged him because faith in God's providence had guarded him from bitterness of soul—**God meant it unto good, to bring to pass, as it is this day, to save much people alive.** Joseph did not understand the events at the time, but he held on to his faith in God. Only later was he able to look back and see the working of God's plan—and that he was an instrument in it.

No matter how much they have been wronged, believers are to be ready to restore relationships with those who have wronged them, look for opportunities to be reconciled to them, and seek to do good toward them.

2. Make Reconciliation a Priority (Matt. 5:23-24)

Instead of arguments, anger, fighting, and killing (vv. 21-22), Jesus showed the proper procedure where differences exist.

Verses 23-24: Therefore if thou bring thy gift to the altar, and there rememberest that thy brother hath aught against thee; ²⁴Leave there thy gift before the altar, and go thy way; first be reconciled to thy brother, and then come and offer thy gift.

Therefore introduces a conclusion based on what Jesus had just said. In essence, our relationship to another Christian **brother** or sister affects our relationship to God. We cannot really worship God if we are at odds with another believer.

Jesus pictured a person on the way to the place of worship, bearing a **gift** to God. When he arrived, he suddenly remembered **that thy brother hath aught against thee.** Notice that the one going to worship had nothing against his Christian brother. In some way, the other had wronged him. But Jesus said that the one who was wronged was to **leave there thy gift before the altar, . . . be reconciled to thy brother, and then come and offer thy gift.** Notice the order. You cannot be right before God until you have become right with your fellow believers.

Being reconciled to someone who has offended you does not mean that he or she will become your closest friend. It does mean, however, "that your relationship will be at least as good as it was before the offense occurred" (Sande, *The Peacemaker*, 198).

In order for this to happen, Ken Sande suggested pursuing reconciliation at three different levels. First, *pursue reconciliation in your thoughts.* Many of us have difficulty not thinking about what someone has done to hurt us, even if we have said "I forgive you." "Try as we might, memories of the offense keep popping back into our minds, and we find ourselves reliving all kinds of painful feelings" (Sande, *The Peacemaker,* 199). For reconciliation at this level, Sande suggested the replacement principle. Every time a negative thought about the experience, event, or person comes into your mind, replace the negative thoughts and memories with positive ones. Since it is very difficult to stop thinking about an unpleasant or hurtful experience, every time you begin to dwell on or brood over what someone has done to you, ask God to help you to think of something about the offender that is good, noble, admirable, lovely, or praiseworthy (Phil. 4:4-7). Then deliberately pray for that person and thank God for him or her.

Second, *pursue reconciliation in your words.* "When talking to others about the person who offended you, make it a point to speak well of the person. Express appreciation for things he or she has done and draw attention to redeeming qualities. Do the same when talking to the offender. Praise, thank, or encourage!" (Sande, *The Peacemaker,* 200-201).

Third, *pursue reconciliation in your deeds.* This is important for two reasons. First, loving actions can change your feelings about a person. As C. S. Lewis noted in his classic book *Mere Christianity* ([New York: Macmillan and Company. 1960], 116), "Don't waste time bothering whether you 'love' your neighbor; act as if you did. As soon as we do this we find one of the great secrets. When you are behaving as if you loved someone, you will presently come to love him." Second, "loving actions can do much more than change your feelings; they can also communicate in unmistakable terms the reality of your forgiveness and your commitment to reconciliation" (Sande, *The Peacemaker,* 202).

There is a beautiful illustration of this principle in the life of Thomas Edison. When Edison and his staff developed the incandescent light bulb, it took hundreds of hours to manufacture a single bulb. One day after finishing a bulb, Edison handed it to a young errand boy and told him to take it upstairs to the testing room. As the boy started up the stairs, he stumbled and fell. The bulb shattered into pieces on the steps. Edison reassured the lad and instructed his staff to begin working on a new bulb. When the bulb was completed several days later, Edison walked over to the same boy, handed him the bulb, and said, "Please take this up to the testing room." The boy didn't deserve to be trusted with the responsibility again, but it was offered to him as though nothing had ever happened. Nothing could have restored the boy to the team or reconciled him to the staff more clearly, quickly, or fully.

Believers must recognize the seriousness of broken relationships. Before they can worship God acceptably, they must seek
to be reconciled—in thought, word, and deed—to people with
whom they have become estranged.

3. Forgive Completely (Col. 3:12-15)

Paul urged his readers to be characterized by distinctively
Christian virtues. They were to forgive one another as Christ
had forgiven them, put on the virtue of love, live in the peace
that Christ gives, and be thankful.

Verses 12-15: **Put on therefore, as the elect of God, holy
and beloved, bowels of mercies, kindness, humbleness of
mind, meekness, long-suffering; [13]Forbearing one another, and forgiving one another, if any man have a quarrel against any: even as Christ forgave you, so also do ye.
[14]And above all these things put on charity, which is the
bond of perfectness. [15]And let the peace of God rule in
your hearts, to the which also ye are called in one body;
and be ye thankful.**

Paul addressed his readers as **the elect of God.** He called
the elect **holy and beloved.** The elect are the objects of God's
love; and **holy** means they are set apart for God's service.

The ancients thought of the **bowels** as the seat of emotions,
much as we think of the heart. As God's people, Paul commanded that they be merciful. **Kindness** renders a Greek word
that means to seek to do good to one who has harmed you. These
Colossian Christians were to be humble and meek also. **Meekness** means "to be teachable." The word was used of training a
horse, the object of which was not to break its spirit but to bring
it under control for service. So **meekness** refers to power under
control. Of course, **long-suffering** means "to suffer long evil
done to you without striking back."

Forbearing one another literally means "holding back." In
this context it means putting up with one another in spite of difficulties. Notice, however, this is a two-way street. Paul added
the reciprocal pronoun **one another.** Others have to put up with

us also. We should bear with one another rather than fussing
and fighting. And if you have been harmed or hurt by another,
you should forgive that person **even as Christ forgave you.**

In verse 14 **charity** renders *agape,* "love." The words **above
all** (*epi pasin*) mean "over all these things." **Bond** denotes a gir-
dle put on over all other clothes to hold them in position. This
bond makes the Christian's clothing complete. The Christlike
behavior expected of Christians grows out of love and is characterized by peace. The best manuscripts read "peace of Christ"
rather than **peace of God.** This **peace** is the peace that Christ
gives to those who believe in Him. The verb rendered **rule**
means to act as an umpire. An umpire serves to preserve order
in any contest. The **body** is the church with Christ as its head.
So Paul called for Christ's peace to dominate a church filled with
tension. This peace gives a positive Christian witness about
Christ and the gospel to the world.

And be ye thankful might appear to be just an after-
thought. Such is hardly the case. An attitude of gratitude pro-
motes peace and harmony in a body of believers. The verb **be**
(*ginesthe*) could be rendered "become." And the present tense
carries the implication that this is a habit that must be ac-
quired. Williams translated the phrase, "And practice being
thankful." Knox suggested, "Learn, too, to be grateful."

And now let us return to verse 13 for a moment. When Paul
wrote **forgiving one another . . . even as Christ forgave
you,** the Greek words he used for **forgiving** (*charizomai*) and
for **forgave** (*echarisato*) come from the root word for "grace"
(*charis*). In other words, forgiveness is an expression of grace
and is not based on whether the forgiven person is deserving of
the forgiveness. The very words used show us that forgiveness is
undeserved and cannot be earned. A good-sense rendering is,
"gracing . . . as Christ graces you." And this takes us to the
heart of this point of the lesson. The standard by which Christians are to forgive those who have wronged them is the forgiveness they have received from Christ.

Have you ever heard someone say—or have you ever said—
"I forgive him [or her]; I just don't want to have anything to do

with him [or her] again"? How would you feel if you had just confessed a sin to the Lord and then you heard Him say, "I forgive you; I just don't want to have anything to do with you again"?

God has given us a high standard to live up to when we have the opportunity to forgive someone. Unfortunately, too many of us do not understand the nature of biblical forgiveness and we practice—or we don't even practice—a form of forgiveness that is neither biblical nor healing. Therefore we need to learn three things that biblical forgiveness is not. First, *biblical forgiveness is not a feeling.* True, we probably will need to change our feelings about someone we need to forgive; but biblical forgiveness is not merely changing how we feel about someone. Neither is biblical forgiveness based on whether we feel like forgiving someone or not. God calls on us to forgive others regardless of our feelings. Second, *biblical forgiveness is not forgetting.* Forgetting is a passive process in which a matter eventually fades from one's memory with the passing of time. Third, *biblical forgiveness is not excusing.* Excusing implies that what one did wasn't really wrong.

What then is biblical forgiveness? Biblical forgiveness is a decision; it is a deliberate act of the will. Biblical forgiveness involves a decision not to think or talk about what someone has done. Biblical forgiveness is an active process; it involves a conscious choice and a deliberate course of action. Biblical forgiveness acknowledges that someone has done something wrong and what that person has done is inexcusable. Nevertheless, one actively chooses to forgive that person anyway.

A woman went to her pastor for advice in dealing with her marriage. When the pastor asked the woman what her complaint was, she replied, "Every time we get into an argument, my husband gets historical." The pastor interrupted the woman and said, "I think you mean *hysterical.*" The woman responded, "No, I mean exactly what I said. My husband keeps a mental record of everything I've ever done wrong; and whenever he's upset, I get a history lesson!"

Too often we keep a record of the wrongs someone has done to us. Too often we bring up past wrongs when we want to hurt

someone or win an argument. When God forgives, He promises
not to keep a record of our sins; He chooses not to mention, re-
count, or think about our sins ever again (Ps. 103:12; 130:3-4;
Isa. 43:25; Jer. 31:34b; Mic. 7:19; 1 Cor. 13:5).

Therefore, as Ken Sande (*The Peacemaker,* 189-199) suggested, biblical forgiveness may be described as a decision to
make four promises:

"I will not think about this incident."

"I will not bring up this incident again and use it
against you."

"I will not talk to others about this incident."

"I will not allow this incident to stand between us or
hinder our personal relationship."

Perhaps you feel that it's not fair. Someone can hurt you, and
you're to forgive that person completely and never bring the matter up again. You're right! It isn't fair. To forgive others genuinely
and completely is difficult. Usually our explanations for not offering forgiveness can be boiled down to three reasons: (a) we withhold forgiveness because we believe the offender must earn or deserve our forgiveness; (b) we want to punish the offender and
make him or her suffer; or (c) we want a guarantee that such an
offense will never occur again. But as Ken Sande again reminded
us, "Forgiveness is based on repentance, not on guarantees." And
again, "we have no right to demand guarantees and withhold forgiveness from a repentant person" (*The Peacemaker,* 194).

Forgiveness is like canceling a debt—it's a costly activity.
When you cancel a debt, the debt doesn't simply disappear.
Rather, you absorb the liability someone else deserved to pay,
and you release the person from liability to punishment—the
punishment of separation and broken relationships.

If you are struggling with forgiving others, recall two things.
First, take another look at your enormous debt that God has forgiven. Too often we take God's forgiveness for granted while we
stubbornly withhold our forgiveness from others. "In effect, we
behave as though others' sins against us are more serious than
our sins against God!" (Sande, *The Peacemaker,* 196). Jesus
warned us against such (Matt. 6:12,14-15). Second, depend on

God's grace and strength to forgive those who have wronged and hurt you. "If you try to forgive others on your own, you are in for a long and frustrating battle" (Sande, *The Peacemaker,* 197).

Corrie ten Boom and her family were arrested by the Nazis during World War II. Her elderly father died shortly thereafter, and Corrie and her sister were sent to a concentration camp. Only Corrie survived, and that by a miracle. After the war, Corrie traveled the world, testifying of God's love. One day at a church in Munich, Germany, she was confronted by the S. S. soldier who stood guard at the shower room door in the processing center at Ravenbruck concentration camp. He came up to her, held out his hand, and said, "How grateful I am for your message, Fraulein, to think that, as you say, He has washed my sins away!"

Corrie said that she tried to raise her hand to take the man's hand, but she could not. She prayed for God to help her, but she still could not raise her arm. She wrote, "I tried to smile, I struggled to raise my hand. I could not. I felt nothing, not the slightest spark of warmth or charity. And so again I breathed a silent prayer. 'Jesus, I cannot forgive him. Give me Your forgiveness.'" Then Corrie wrote, "As I took his hand the most incredible thing happened. From my shoulder along my arm and through my hand a current seemed to pass from me to him, while into my heart sprang a love for this stranger that almost overwhelmed me. So I discovered that it is not on our forgiveness any more than on our goodness that the world's healing hinges, but on Him. When He tells us to love our enemies, He gives, along with the command, the love itself" (*The Hiding Place* [New York: Bantam Books, 1974], 238).

As believers, in any and every conflict, we must be ready to restore relationships, make reconciliation a priority, and forgive completely. This is the culmination of the peacemaking process God intends for His people to apply in their homes, workplaces, churches, neighborhoods, and anywhere else they experience personal conflict with others. May God bless you as you seek to be a peacemaker for Him.

STUDY THEME: FINDING SECURITY
IN A TURBULENT WORLD

August 2

TRUE OR FALSE SECURITY?

Background Scripture: Jeremiah 1:1–2:28; 5:1-31
Focal Verses: Jeremiah 1:1-3,17-19; 2:12-13,27-28;
5:30-31

INTRODUCTION

1. This is the first of five lessons on the study theme "Finding Security in a Turbulent World."

2. We live in a time of crisis and transition as we approach a new century and a new millennium. Many adults are overwhelmed by fear as they face an uncertain future. All are seeking security, but many are confused by the variety of ways proposed to find security. These five lessons, drawn from the Book of Jeremiah, are designed to help adults find true and lasting security in God.

3. These five lessons will not provide a study of the entire Book of Jeremiah. Rather, they will focus on significant portions of the book related to "Finding Security in a Turbulent World." All the lessons deal with contrasting approaches to finding security. This first lesson focuses on the basic contrast between true and false security. The only true and lasting security is found in God; all other things around which people build their lives provide only an illusion of security.

4. The Life Question is, Where can I find security in a turbulent world?

5. The Lesson Bible Truth is that God provides the only real and lasting security.

6. The Lesson Outcome is to help you commit yourself to God as the only real source of security.

I. SOME PRELIMINARY CONSIDERATIONS

1. A Turbulent World

As we shall see, Jeremiah lived a turbulent life in a turbulent time in history. Every age has its claim to be a turbulent time. When Charles Dickens began his famous novel *A Tale of Two Cities,* he wrote: "It was the best of times, it was the worst of times, it was the age of wisdom, it was the age of foolishness, it was the epoch of belief, it was the epoch of incredulity, it was the season of Light, it was the season of Darkness, it was the spring of hope, it was the winter of despair." Dickens wrote over two generations after the events of the French Revolution, but he said that the same words fit his own time (*Complete Works* [New York: Oxford University Press, n.d.], 1). We could apply the same words to the closing years of the 20th century.

2. Search for Security

Human beings have sought security since the beginning of time. People especially become concerned about security during times of crises or transition. Unfortunately, many adults have placed their trust in such things as success, pleasure, themselves, their families, and so forth. When the ultimate tests of life come, people often turn in vain to God or to their gods for help. Christian adults have discovered that God offers the only source for true and lasting security. He provides security for this life and for the life beyond death.

II. FOCAL VERSES EXAMINED
(Jer. 1:1-3,17-19; 2:12-13,27-28; 5:30-31)

The Scriptures for this week's lesson come from the biblical account of Jeremiah's call and his early sermons. Jeremiah was called during a turbulent time (Jer. 1:1-3). God warned him of the difficulty of his mission but promised to be with him (Jer. 1:17-19). Jeremiah condemned the people of Judah for turning

from God to idols that would be unable to help them in times
of need (Jer. 2:12-13,27-28). Jeremiah blamed not only the people but also the religious leaders for the popularity of moral corruption and idolatry (Jer. 5:30-31).

1. A Turbulent Age (Jer. 1:1-3)

These verses introduce the Book of Jeremiah by answering
three important questions: (1) Who was Jeremiah? (2) What was
his mission? (3) When did he serve?

Verses 1-3: **The words of Jeremiah the son of Hilkiah, of
the priests that were in Anathoth in the land of Benjamin: ²To whom the word of the LORD came in the days of
Josiah the son of Amon king of Judah, in the thirteenth
year of his reign. ³It came also in the days of Jehoiakim
the son of Josiah king of Judah, unto the end of the
eleventh year of Zedekiah the son of Josiah king of
Judah, unto the carrying away of Jerusalem captive in
the fifth month.**

Jeremiah was **the son of** a priest named **Hilkiah** [hil-
KIGH-uh], a different Hilkiah than the one who discovered the
book of the law in the temple (2 Kings 22:8). Jeremiah's father
was from the town of **Anathoth** [AN-uh-thawth], about three
miles northeast of Jerusalem, in the part of Israel originally
given to the tribe of **Benjamin**. We know nothing else about
Jeremiah's father, but we may assume that Hilkiah was one of
the few godly priests of the time who raised his son in the ways
of the Lord.

Jeremiah was set apart by God from before his birth to be a
prophet (1:4-5). His call came **in the thirteenth year . . . of
Josiah king of Judah.** This was 627 B.C. Jeremiah's call is described, as are the calls of so many Old Testament prophets, by
the words **the word of the LORD came.** Jeremiah did not
choose to be a prophet; God chose Jeremiah to be a prophet.
Like all true prophets, Jeremiah was called by God to deliver
God's word to the people, not to share his own thoughts, ideas,
and recommendations.

Since Jeremiah spoke of himself as just a child when he was called (1:6) and since he served for over 40 years (1:2-3), he was probably less than 20 when he was called. If so, Jeremiah was born under the long and wicked reign of Manasseh [muh-NASS-uh], whose sins sealed the fate of Judah (2 Kings 21:1-18).

King Manasseh's evil policies were continued by his son **Amon** [AM-uhn] (2 Kings 21:19-26). **Amon** was succeeded by his **son Josiah,** the last good king of Judah. Josiah made a valiant attempt to revive the faith of Judah and to turn them from their idolatry, but he met a tragic death while still a young man (2 Kings 22:1-23:30). Following Josiah's death, a series of evil kings came to the throne. Much of Jeremiah's preaching was done during the reign of the evil **Jehoiakim** [jih-HOY-uh-kim], an implacable enemy of the prophet. Jeremiah continued to preach until the **end of the eleventh year of Zedekiah** [zed-uh-KIGH-uh] **son of Josiah king of Judah, unto the carrying away of Jerusalem captive in the fifth month.** This was when Jeremiah's chief prophecy came true in 587 B.C.—when Nebuchadnezzar [neb-yoo-kad-NEZ-uhr], king of Babylon, captured Jerusalem, killed many, and carried the best of the survivors as exiles to Babylon.

Thus it was that during the time of Jeremiah, the Assyrian Empire, which had terrorized the ancient world for years, fell to the Babylonians. Then Judah, after a few years of relative stability, was caught in the middle of a power struggle between Babylon and Egypt. The kings of Judah kept looking to Egypt, which helped lead to their destruction. This is a military-political explanation of the cause of Judah's ruin; however, Jeremiah insisted that Judah's real problems were not political, military, and economic but moral and spiritual. The people had turned from God, their only source of life and security.

Writing of Jeremiah's time of ministry, F. B. Huey, Jr. wrote: "The closing years of the seventh century B.C. proved to be a turbulent era in the ANE [Ancient Near East]. That time can only be described as a time of crisis and transition" ("Jeremiah," in *The New American Commentary,* vol. 16 [Nashville: Broadman Press, 1993], 19).

Every generation can lay claim to being a turbulent age. One of my ancestors fought at the Battle of Lexington in 1775. My great-grandfather fought in the Civil War, and my grandfather was born in the midst of that war. My parents were born in the optimistic first decade of the 20th century, but they were children when the whole world went to war from 1914–1918. My wife and I were born in the midst of the Great Depression; and our children were born during the years of the Cold War, when nuclear war with Soviet Russia threatened the earth.

Each of these times was turbulent. Now we are counting down toward the launch of a new century and a new millennium. Many people are focused on the financial, political, military, technological, and vocational aspects of the unknown 21st century. Jeremiah calls us to hear the ever-relevant message that God spoke through him to an earlier turbulent age. Without God, we are not ready for anything; with God, we are ready for everything.

2. Finding True Security (Jer. 1:17-19)

These verses should be read with verses 4-10, which describe Jeremiah's call. God did not sugarcoat the difficulties Jeremiah would face in proclaiming God's word in that turbulent age. Allied against him would be **the kings of Judah . . . the princes . . . the priests . . . and . . . the people of the land** (v. 18). Later references show that the prophets also were among the implacable foes of Jeremiah. Who was on Jeremiah's side? With the exception of his friend and secretary Baruch [BEHR-uhk], Jeremiah had few who supported him—other than God.

Verses 17-19: **Thou therefore gird up thy loins, and arise, and speak unto them all that I command thee: be not dismayed at their faces, lest I confound thee before them. [18]For, behold, I have made thee this day a defensed city, and an iron pillar, and brazen walls against the whole land, against the kings of Judah, against the princes thereof, against the priests thereof, and against**

the people of the land. ¹⁹And they shall fight against thee;
but they shall not prevail against thee; for I am with thee,
saith the LORD, to deliver thee.

Verse 17 contains a threefold challenge: (1) **Gird up thy
loins** means "Get yourself ready!" (NIV). In Jeremiah's time,
men wore long robes. When they performed strenuous activities,
they had to tie up their long robes to free their legs for action.
(2) **Speak unto them all that I command thee.** This repeats
what God told Jeremiah when earlier he had complained that he
was too young to be a prophet (1:6-7). (3) **Be not dismayed at
their faces.** This also repeats an earlier challenge (1:8a). The
faces of Jeremiah's enemies would show all kinds of negative
emotions—from ridicule to murderous hatred. God warned Jeremiah of this ahead of time. God also warned His prophet that
He would allow Jeremiah to be terrified if he gave in to the
threats of his enemies.

Verses 18-19 contain a threefold promise. First, God used
three comparisons to promise strength to Jeremiah. God
promised to make the prophet like **a defensed city**—that is,
like "a fortified city" (NIV)—like **an iron pillar,** and like
brazen walls—that is, like "a bronze wall" (NIV). Second, God
promised, **They shall fight against thee; but they shall not
prevail against thee.** Jeremiah was about to go to the front in
a war zone. He would be under constant attack by overwhelming enemy forces, who seemed sure to win. However, God assured Jeremiah that His side would win. Third, God promised,
I am with thee . . . to deliver thee. This repeated the earlier
promise of verse 8. God did not promise to **deliver** Jeremiah
from passing through difficult times; the Lord promised to be
with Jeremiah as he passed through them. Later Jeremiah
often recalled these challenges and promises.

Although the prophet Jeremiah lived a turbulent life in turbulent times, the Lord provided him true and lasting security.
Even as God promised strength and ultimate security to Jeremiah, so does He promise the same to those who trust Him in
our turbulent world.

3. Folly of False Security (Jer. 2:12-13,27-28)

The sermons of Jeremiah 2–6 represent Jeremiah's earliest preaching. They likely were preached during the reign of Josiah. Although Jeremiah was sympathetic with Josiah's attempts to revive Judah's faith, the sermons of these early chapters paint a bleak picture of the real moral and spiritual state of the nation.

Verses 12-13: **Be astonished, O ye heavens, at this, and be horribly afraid, be ye very desolate, saith the LORD. ¹³For my people have committed two evils; they have forsaken me the fountain of living waters, and hewed them out cisterns, broken cisterns, that can hold no water.**

Jeremiah 2 is in the form of legal charges brought by God against Judah. After describing what God had done to bless His people, God asked if any nation had done what Judah had done in forsaking their god. He called on the **heavens** to **be astonished . . . be horribly afraid . . .** and **be . . . very desolate** because of the twofold sins of Judah. Verse 13 spells out their **two evils.** The people of Judah had **forsaken** the Lord, who was like **the fountain of living waters** ("the spring of living water," NIV) and had dug for themselves **cisterns, broken cisterns, that can hold no water.**

J. A. Thompson (*The Book of Jeremiah,* in The New International Commentary on the Old Testament [Grand Rapids: William B. Eerdmans Publishing Company, 1980], 171) stated the meaning plainly: "The symbolism was clear to the people of Judah. Every landowner could wish to have a flowing spring on his property, which would obviate his having to dig a cistern in the limestone hills. To ensure that it held water he had to plaster inside with lime plaster. He would then direct rainwater into it when the rain came. But such cisterns built into limestone rock developed cracks and the water seeped out, leaving the farmer without the precious life-giving commodity."

Water from cisterns was tepid compared to water from a fresh-water spring. And if the cistern leaked, even the tepid water leaked out. This illustrates the twofold folly of Judah's idolatry. They had forsaken a spring of fresh water for a cistern of stale water; and when they needed the stale water, the cistern held no water at all. Thus when the people went to their gods for life-giving sustenance, they found none.

Verses 27-28: **Saying to a stock, Thou art my father; and to a stone, Thou hast brought me forth: for they have turned their back unto me, and not their face: but in the time of their trouble they will say, Arise, and save us. ²⁸But where are thy gods that thou hast made thee? let them arise, if they can save thee in the time of thy trouble: for according to the number of thy cities are thy gods, O Judah.**

These verses further illustrate the folly of placing security in idols. God's charge was directed against the kings, princes, priests, and prophets (2:26). God accused them of placing their trust in gods of **stock** (or "wood," NIV) and **stone.** The people of Judah honored these gods, which they themselves had made, as if the idols had given them life. In doing so, the people had **turned their back** on the Lord, who was the true Giver of life and sustenance.

However, when trouble came, the people inevitably would call out to the Lord, **Arise, and save us.** God taunted them by asking, **But where are thy gods that thou hast made thee?** God asked **if** these gods could **save** them **in the time of their trouble.** The answer was obvious. Pieces of wood and stone could not save them.

Today's sophisticated worshipers of false gods would never worship some grotesque image of an ancient god, but they are just as guilty as the people of Judah in Jeremiah's day. People's true gods are those things that they give their primary attention to and that they strive the most for—be they pleasures, successes, possessions, power, fame, families, health, and so on. Whether people realize it or not, these are the gods that have taken the place that should be reserved for the one true and living God.

These modern idolaters may even claim to trust in God, but the real test comes when life crashes in on them—as it does on everyone at times—and they realize they need help beyond what they can provide for themselves. Nothing is so sad as a self-sufficient person at an accident site, in intensive care, or in a funeral home. Their gods offer them no help or security when they most need it. At such times, many people call out the name of God. And even though it may sound callous on God's part, according to this passage God in essence says, "They have their own gods; let those gods help them." Or, "They made their own beds; let them sleep in them."

Security is a big word for all of us. We put various words in front of it. We speak of financial security, job security, and even national security. Yet millions have learned that financial security is an illusion. Job security can disappear with the next downsizing. And even national security is not a biblical promise. Hebrews 12:26-28 describes how God will shake all things and all things other than His kingdom will fall apart. Why then should we place our trust in what, when shaken, will surely fall apart—when we could place our trust in that which will withstand any shaking? Such a choice is sinful and foolish. Ultimately, any substitute will fail to provide the security you sought.

4. Popularity of False Security (Jer. 5:30-31)

God challenged Jeremiah to find in the city one just man who sought the truth, promising to spare the city if the prophet found such a man (5:1). Unable to find such a man among the common people, Jeremiah felt that surely he could find one among the city's leading citizens; however, he found none (5:4-5). Chapter 5 builds to a crescendo in verses 30-31 where both leaders and people are condemned.

Verses 30-31: **A wonderful and horrible thing is committed in the land; ³¹The prophets prophesy falsely, and the priests bear rule by their means; and my people love to have it so: and what will ye do in the end thereof?**

The Hebrew word translated **wonderful** means "astonishing." Jeremiah used it of astonishment at the **horrible thing . . . committed in the land.** The *New International Version* reads, "A horrible and shocking thing has happened in the land." Jeremiah was by no means the only prophet in Judah. There were multitudes of **prophets** and **priests.** Unfortunately, God said, **The prophets prophesy falsely.** These men who claimed to speak God's truth spoke only lies. God also condemned the priests. In the words **the priests bear rule by their means,** translators are not sure whether **their** refers to the prophets or to the priests. Thus some translations understand it to mean "the priests rule by their own authority" (NIV; similarly, NASB) while other translations understand it to mean the "priests rule as the prophets command" (TEV; similarly, NRSV). In either case, both groups of religious leaders were part of the problem, not part of the cure.

To make matters worse, God said, **My people love to have it so.** Instead of protesting the corruption of their religious leaders, the people were glad to have prophets who preached what they wanted to hear and to have priests who assured them that performing their outward religious duties was enough. No wonder God asked these corrupt leaders and people, **What will ye do in the end?**

People don't like to be forced to face that question. Some have become so skilled at self-deception that they have convinced themselves that all will be well for them when the end comes. Others, however, occasionally have moments of truth or of divine conviction when they shudder at the thought. But such moments usually pass quickly, and they turn up the volume on the sound track of their evil lives to drown out the voice of conscience or of God.

Centuries ago Geoffrey Chaucer asked, "If gold rust, what shall iron do?" He answered his question by saying,

> For if a priest be foul in whom we trust,
> No wonder if a common man should rust!

("Prologue," *The Canterbury Tales,* in *Handbook of Preaching Resources from English Literature,* compiled and edited by James Douglas Robertson [New York: The Macmillan Company, 1962], 152.)

Where and to what are you looking to find security in your turbulent world?

August 9

FEELING SECURE OR BEING SECURE?

Background Scripture: Jeremiah 7:1-15
Focal Verses: Jeremiah 7:1-15

INTRODUCTION

1. This lesson focuses on attempts to worship God through what amount to nothing more than empty worship practices. People who do this may feel secure because they think they are building their security on God, but true security comes only when our worship is real.

2. Hence the Life Question is, How can I be sure my faith is in God and not based on empty religious practices that only help me feel secure?

3. The Lesson Bible Truth is that real security in a turbulent world comes not through empty religious practices but through genuine worship of God that strengthens the relationship with Him and affects how the worshiper lives.

4. The Lesson Outcome is to help you experience real security through worship of God that strengthens your relationship with Him and affects how you live.

I. SOME PRELIMINARY CONSIDERATIONS

1. The Contemporary Context

Often during times of turmoil, people turn to religion for security. However, turning to religion may not be the same as turning to God. Some people place their trust in observance of religious practices. Some of these are even regular churchgoers. People can go to church every time the doors are open; and unless their churchgoing is reflected in how they live each day, their trust in churchgoing is deceptive. Many others in our culture trust in a kind of civil religion. They go to church from time to time; they profess to believe in God; they observe special days like Christmas, Easter, and Thanksgiving; they believe that God has His hand on America and Americans. Both the regular churchgoer and the irregular churchgoer are fooling only themselves with their feelings that they are secure. Only those who truly worship God and truly live for Him know the God who offers real security.

2. Jeremiah's Temple Sermon

Jeremiah 7:1-15 is crucial to understanding Jeremiah. The actions and words of Jeremiah at the temple gate took place early in his ministry and set the tone for all that followed. These verses deal with the so-called temple sermon. Jeremiah showed himself to be a man who was unafraid to speak God's word. He went to the sacred temple and condemned the nation's blatant hypocrisy. He did this at a time when the political and religious leaders were encouraging people to trust in the presence of the temple as assurance that God would protect them—no matter what.

II. FOCAL VERSES EXAMINED (Jer. 7:1-15)

According to James Leo Green, Jeremiah 7:1-15 has the form of a legal brief. Verses 1-4 state the prosecution's case. Verses 5-7 state God's laws. Verses 8-11 summarize the verdict. Verses 12-15 declare the punishment ("Jeremiah," in *The Broadman Bible Commentary*, vol. 6 [Nashville: Broadman Press, 1971], 62).

1. Don't Be Deceived (Jer. 7:1-4)

People need to avoid the deception that placing their faith in religious institutions and on religious practices brings security in a turbulent world.

Verses 1-2: **The word that came to Jeremiah from the LORD, saying, ²Stand in the gate of the LORD's house, and**

**proclaim there this word, and say, Hear the word of the
Lord, all ye of Judah, that enter in at these gates to worship the Lord.**

Many times in the Book of Jeremiah, we read that God's
word . . . came to Jeremiah. On this particular occasion, the
Lord told the prophet to **stand in the gate of the Lord's
house.** The similarity of Jeremiah 7:1-15 to Jeremiah 26:1-7
has caused most Bible students to identify these as the same
event. Jeremiah 26:1 says that it took place in the early part of
the reign of King Jehoiakim [jih-HOY-uh-kim]. Much of Jeremiah's preaching took place during Jehoiakim's reign (609–598
B.C.). Jeremiah's temple sermon explains why the two became
implacable enemies. Following the temple sermon, the leaders,
including the king, wanted to kill Jeremiah (Jer. 26:7-24).

Jeremiah was to speak unto **all ye** ("people," NIV) **of Judah.**
Because the temple in Jerusalem was the central sanctuary, Jeremiah was stationed at a place where he would be heard by
people from all over Judah. News of what was said there would
be spread throughout the land by word of mouth.

Supposedly, the people came **to worship.** That was the crux
of the issue. Did they truly **worship** the Lord? The word **worship** pictures someone bowing down in genuine reverence before
the Lord. Those who truly worshiped acknowledged God's lord-
ship over not just the temple but over all of life. Israel's
covenant with the Lord included not only worship in the sanctuary but also obedience to God's commandments.

***Verses 3-4:* Thus saith the Lord of hosts, the God of Is-
rael, Amend your ways and your doings, and I will cause
you to dwell in this place. ⁴Trust ye not in lying words,
saying, The temple of the Lord, The temple of the Lord,
The temple of the Lord, are these.**

This was probably the first time many of the people had seen
the young prophet. If so, they must have been shocked when he
told them in the name of **the Lord of hosts, the God of Israel, Amend your ways and your doings. Amend** means
"make good." Thus instead of greeting these self-satisfied people
as they were entering the Lord's house, the young prophet, in

essence, told them to clean up their act. If they did, the Lord promised, **I will cause you to dwell in this place.** The word **place** sometimes referred to the temple and sometimes to the land. It is hard to determine which Jeremiah meant.

Even harsher words followed when the Lord said, **Trust ye not in lying words.** The word **trust** is the usual Hebrew word for placing one's faith in something, thus making it the basis for their security. They were placing their security in **lying** or "deceptive" (NIV) **words.** J. A. Thompson (*The Book of Jeremiah,* 277) translated it "The Lie." What was "The Lie"? The clue is in the threefold repetition of **the temple of the LORD** that they recited as a kind of spiritual good luck charm or magic formula: "This is the temple of the LORD, the temple of the LORD, the temple of the LORD" (NIV).

These words reflect what is called temple theology. Basically, the people of Judah believed that God had promised to protect and preserve His temple, His city, and His people from all dangers. They based their doctrines on Scriptures in which God called Israel as His chosen people. They felt that these promises were tested once and for all when the Assyrians had threatened Jerusalem during the time of Isaiah the prophet and Hezekiah [HEZ-ih-kigh-uh] the king (Isa. 36–37; 2 Kings 18–19; 2 Chron. 32).

What the people had was presumption based on a lie, not genuine trust based on the truth. Jeremiah dared to confront them with the truth. Jeremiah identified this thinking as a lie because it was based on recalling only God's promises while ignoring His warnings and the conditions for the promises. Just because the people continued to go through the motions of worship in the temple did not mean they were obeying God. The test of whether their worship was genuine was how they lived day by day.

In our century, the Titanic has become a striking symbol of misplaced confidence and false feelings of security. Those who sailed on the Titanic were assured that the ship was unsinkable. So strongly did the ship's owners believe this claim that the Titanic carried only enough lifeboats for a fraction of the passen-

gers and crew. But the Titanic struck an iceberg in just the right
way that it ripped a huge gash down one side, and the unsinkable ship sank with great loss of life.

Feelings of security are not enough. In fact, if these feelings
are based on lies and half-truths, such feelings can lull us into a
complacency that proves deadly.

2. Change Your Ways (Jer. 7:5-7)

Jeremiah told the people they needed to change their ways by
forsaking their sins against God, against one another, and
against helpless people.

**Verses 5-7: For if ye thoroughly amend your ways and
your doings; if ye thoroughly execute judgment between
a man and his neighbor; ⁶if ye oppress not the stranger,
the fatherless, and the widow, and shed not innocent
blood in this place, neither walk after other gods to your
hurt: ⁷then will I cause you to dwell in this place, in the
land that I gave to your fathers, forever and ever.**

Thoroughly amend your ways is, literally, "If amending
you amend," and **thoroughly execute judgment** means "if
executing you execute justice" (Andrew W. Blackwood, Jr.,
Commentary on Jeremiah [Waco: Word Books, Publisher, 1977],
91). The idea in **thoroughly** is "if in very fact you do." (Thompson, *The Book of Jeremiah,* 277). The people needed to make
changes or corrections in their actions, and this involved stopping what they had been doing and acting according to God's
commandments.

Execute judgment between a man and his neighbor
points to a basic area of needed change. **Judgment** translates
the Hebrew word for "justice" (NASB), which is common in the
Old Testament. The word means to treat others right. *Today's
English Version* translates the exhortation, "Be fair in your
treatment of one another." Jeremiah cited an example of what
he meant: **oppress not the stranger, the fatherless, and the
widow.** These three groups represented the helpless groups in
ancient Israelite society. The **stranger** was a resident alien,

"someone who because of war, famine, plague, blood-guiltiness, or other misfortunes had to leave his original home or tribe and seek shelter at another place" (Thompson, *The Book of Jeremiah,* 278.) The Old Testament often linked these misplaced persons with orphans and widows as groups toward whom the Israelites were to "deal with . . . justly" (NIV).

The warning against shedding **innocent blood** may refer to child sacrifice, but it probably referred to legalized murder. The people in authority—including the evil kings—often used the courts to condemn and execute their political enemies and other people they wanted killed (see 2 Kings 24:4).

Walk after other gods shows their basic sin. The gods of other peoples seldom made any moral demands on their followers. In fact, some pagan religions promoted sin as part of their worship. The religion of Israel often is called ethical monotheism to stress its two primary distinctives: belief in one God who demands that His people be holy as He is holy.

The Lord God promised that **if** His people changed their ways by stopping their sins and beginning to do right, **then will I cause you to dwell in this place,** which here referred to **the land** God gave to the Israelites' forefathers for **forever and ever.**

Jeremiah, therefore, called the people back to the basics of their faith. All was not yet hopeless. They could repent of their sins and change their ways.

3. Practice What You Profess (Jer. 7:8-11)

Verses 5-7 state what God expected and demanded. Verses 8-11 present God's accusation that the people were doing just the opposite of what He commanded.

Verses 8-10: **Behold, ye trust in lying words, that cannot profit. ⁹Will ye steal, murder, and commit adultery, and swear falsely, and burn incense unto Baal, and walk after other gods whom ye know not; ¹⁰and come and stand before me in this house, which is called by my name, and say, We are delivered to do all these abominations?**

Verse 8 is almost a restatement of the first part of verse 4. The difference is that in verse 4 Jeremiah warned the people of Judah against trusting in lying words, and in verse 8 he accused them of actually trusting in **lying words. Cannot profit** is an understatement for emphasis. This lie was more than useless; it was deadly and would eventually destroy them if they did not repent and place their trust in the Lord.

In verses 9-10 Jeremiah, in essence, asked them, "Do you dare to commit the worst of sins and then come to worship in the temple and claim that you are safe no matter how you live?" Verse 9 begins with God, through Jeremiah, accusing the people of breaking many of the Ten Commandments: **steal, murder, . . . commit adultery, . . . swear falsely**—the Eighth, Sixth, Seventh, and Ninth Commandments. By burning **incense unto Baal** and walking **after other gods,** they broke the First Commandment also. By thinking they would remake God into their own image and use His name to cover their hypocrisy, they broke the Second and Third Commandments. They committed all these horrible sins and then had the gall to **come and stand before** God in the **house . . . called by** His **name.** As they did, these blatant hypocrites dared to say, **We are delivered to do all these abominations.** Or, "'We are safe'—safe to do all these detestable things" (NIV).

The Bible uses strong language to warn people who think they can live as they please just because they go through the motions of worshiping God. The prophets were particularly outspoken against this dangerous form of self-deception (1 Sam. 15:22; Isa. 1:10-17; Amos 5:21-25). The most scathing words of Jesus were directed at religious hypocrites (Matt. 23). Some hypocrites are fully aware of their hypocrisy. Others merely deceive themselves into feeling secure in spite of continuing to practice sin. They trust such things as their church membership, their baptism, their parents' religion, or their participation on special holidays.

Verse 11: **Is this house, which is called by my name, become a den of robbers in your eyes? Behold, even I have seen it, saith the LORD.**

God, through the prophet, continued His questions. Did they intend to make God's **house** into **a den of robbers? Robbers** often used caves as hide-outs from which they ventured forth to commit their crimes. In Jeremiah's day, the hypocrites who ventured forth from the temple to live their evil lives returned to the temple in the same way that thieves returned to their den.

Verse 11 closes on an ominous note. Robbers depend on no one knowing the location of their den. But God said, **I have seen it.** These ancient people must have accepted as fact the sentiment behind Charles Churchill's words:

> Keep up appearances; there lies the test;
> The world will give thee credit for the rest.
> Outward be fair, however foul within;
> Sin, if thou wilt; but then, in secret, sin.
> This maxim's into common favor grown,
> Vice is no longer vice unless 'tis known.

("Night," in James Douglas Robertson, *Handbook of Preaching Resources from English Literature,* 92.)

4. Heed God's Warnings (Jer. 7:12-15)

Following the accusations in verses 8-11 came the pronouncement of the punishment in verses 12-15.

Verses 12-15: **But go ye now unto my place which was in Shiloh, where I set my name at the first, and see what I did to it for the wickedness of my people Israel.** [13]**And now, because ye have done all these works, saith the** LORD**, and I spake unto you, rising up early and speaking, but ye heard not; and I called you, but ye answered not;** [14]**therefore will I do unto this house, which is called by my name, wherein ye trust, and unto the place which I gave to you and to your fathers, as I have done to Shiloh.** [15]**And I will cast you out of my sight, as I have cast out all your brethren, even the whole seed of Ephraim.**

God warned the people to learn the lessons of history. First, He pointed them to the fate of **Shiloh** (vv. 12-14) and then to the fate of **Ephraim** (v. 15).

God called Shiloh **my place . . . where I set my name at
the first. Shiloh** had been the location of the tabernacle in Israel's early years in the promised land after the conquest (Josh.
18:1). The tabernacle was still there when Eli and Samuel min-
istered as priests (1 Sam. 1:3; 3:1,21). God challenged those who
felt secure in the temple to visit the ruins at Shiloh and **see
what** He **did to it for the wickedness of** His **people Israel.**
Shiloh apparently was destroyed by the Philistines after the
battle described in 1 Samuel 4.

God warned that the temple, in which the people of Jeremiah's
day trusted, would meet the same fate for the same reasons. God
repeatedly had called Judah to repent. In verse 13 God is pictured as persistently calling. He is like someone **rising up early**
in the morning and calling throughout the day. In spite of God's
longsuffering love, the people had **heard not.** He had **called**
them, but they **answered not.** Therefore the Lord said He would
do unto this house in Jerusalem what He had **done to Shiloh.**

The Lord then cited a more recent example of divine judgment
on His people for their sins and impenitence. **Ephraim** was the
name by which the Northern Kingdom of Israel was known. Not
much more than a century earlier, God had sent the Assyrians to
defeat the 10 northern tribes and to carry the survivors into captivity. If God had done this to these **brethren** of the people of
Judah, they could expect the same judgment for the same sins.

Someone has said that people who ignore history's lessons are
doomed to repeat them. Unless Judah learned from the fate of
Shiloh and **Ephraim,** they too would end up on the scrap heap
of history. The people of both of these former places had pre-
sumed that God would spare them simply because they were
His people. But God had not spared them. Neither would He
spare Judah. Before the end of Jeremiah's life and the lives of
many who heard his temple sermon, Nebuchadnezzar [neb-yoo-
kad-NEZ-uhr] would defeat Judah, destroy the temple, and
carry most of the survivors into exile in Babylon.

And what about you? Do you just *feel* secure? Or are you *really*
secure? On what are you basing your security? And does it make
any difference in how you live?

August 16

TRUE OR FALSE MESSENGERS?

Background Scripture: Jeremiah 28:1-17
Focal Verses: Jeremiah 28:1-2,5-13,15-17

INTRODUCTION

1. This is the third lesson on "Finding Security in a Turbulent World." It focuses on false messengers. The danger of false messengers is that they speak lies that form the basis for people to place their security in something other than God.

2. Thus an important question is, How can I decide if a person who claims to have a message from God is speaking the truth?

3. The Lesson Bible Truth is that since not everyone who claims to speak for God is a true messenger, God's people must use discernment in deciding whom to believe.

4. The Lesson Outcome is to help you develop a sense of spiritual discernment so you will reject false messengers who claim to speak for God and heed true messengers.

I. SOME PRELIMINARY CONSIDERATIONS

1. The Contemporary Context

We hear many voices making various claims. All claim to speak the truth, whether politicians, salespeople, preachers, psychics, or futurists. How can we tell who is telling the truth, especially when the message relates to moral and spiritual issues? We need to learn how to recognize true messengers of God and to build our lives on the God whose truth they proclaim.

2. Prophet Versus Prophet

Jeremiah 28 records a dramatic confrontation between two men—each of whom claimed to be speaking for God but who

delivered opposite messages. Jeremiah preached that God was
sending the Babylonians as His instruments of judgment on
wicked Judah. Jeremiah declared that Judah's only security
lay in entrusting themselves to and obeying God. Hananiah
[han-uh-NIGH-uh], Jeremiah's antagonist, declared with great
confidence the popular message that God would deliver Judah
from the Babylonians in a short amount of time. Most of the
people believed this lie and eventually paid the price for this
false security.

II.   FOCAL VERSES EXAMINED (Jer. 28:1-2,5-13,15-17)

Jeremiah 27 and 28 belong together. These two chapters describe Jeremiah's reaction to a coalition of small nations, including Judah, in the Syria-Palestine area who tried to oppose
Babylon. This situation led to the prophecy of Hananiah, one of
the false prophets.

1. Popular or True? (Jer. 28:1-2)

One of the challenges of studying the Book of Jeremiah is de-
termining when each event happened. This difficulty is because
the chapters are not arranged in the order of events. Jeremiah
began his ministry when Josiah was king and served during the
reigns of four other kings. The fourth and last of the kings of
Judah was Zedekiah [zed-uh-KIGH-uh], who ruled from
597–587 B.C.

Verses 1-2: **And it came to pass the same year, in the beginning of the reign of Zedekiah king of Judah, in the
fourth year, and in the fifth month, that Hananiah the
son of Azur the prophet, which was of Gibeon, spake unto
me in the house of the LORD, in the presence of the priests
and of all the people, saying, ²Thus speaketh the LORD of
hosts, the God of Israel, saying, I have broken the yoke of
the king of Babylon.**

The events described in chapter 28 took place **in the beginning of the reign of Zedekiah.** The Hebrews divided a king's

reign into two parts or halves. **The beginning** here means "in the first half of his reign." Thus **the beginning** in this case is further defined as **the fourth year.** According to Charles Lee Feinberg ("Jeremiah," in *The Expositor's Bible Commentary,* vol. 6 [Grand Rapids: William B. Eerdmans Publishing Company, 1986], 547) this would have been in 594-593 B.C.

The same year refers back to the events of chapter 27. In this chapter Jeremiah placed a wooden yoke on his neck and prophesied that Nebuchadnezzar, king of Babylon, would place a yoke on the necks of Judah and surrounding nations. Jeremiah further declared that God was using Nebuchadnezzar as an instrument of divine judgment and that failing to submit to the Babylonian yoke would be the same as rebellion against God. God had revealed to Jeremiah that the Jews would spend 70 years in the Babylonian captivity.

Hananiah confronted Jeremiah **in the house of the LORD, in the presence of the priests and of all the people.** Although **Hananiah** is mentioned only in this chapter, he claimed to be a **prophet.** He certainly spoke like one. He began his message in the impressive style of a prophet by declaring, **Thus speaketh the LORD of hosts, the God of Israel.** Hananiah even used the tense used by prophets to speak of future events as if the events already had happened—**I have broken the yoke of the king of Babylon.**

Did Hananiah intend to mislead the people, or did he sincerely believe he was speaking the truth? He certainly went out on a limb when he set an exact time ("two full years," vv. 3,11) for the return of the temple treasuries and the king who was taken to Babylon by Nebuchadnezzar in 597 B.C. ("Jeconiah" [jek-oh-NIGH-uh], v. 4, is another name for King Jehoiachin [jih-HOY-uh-kin].) At any rate, Hananiah's message certainly was the one the people wanted to hear.

Hananiah's message was certainly more popular to the people of Judah than Jeremiah's message. To most of them, Jeremiah seemed not only a false prophet but a coward and a traitor to his nation. But Jeremiah followed in a long line of God's prophets who in their day stood alone and declared God's truth.

Many people still judge messengers and their messages on the basis of their popularity. But truth is often unpopular, and true prophets often stand virtually alone. In trying to distinguish true prophets from false prophets, beware of prophets who seem popular and tell people what they want to hear. More often than not, true prophets speak what is unpopular—yet true.

2. Pleasing or Proven? (Jer. 28:5-9)

Jeremiah responded to Hananiah in the temple before the same groups mentioned in verse 1.

Verses 5-6: **Then the prophet Jeremiah said unto the prophet Hananiah in the presence of the priests, and in the presence of all the people that stood in the house of the LORD, ⁶Even the prophet Jeremiah said, Amen: the LORD do so: the LORD perform thy words which thou hast prophesied, to bring again the vessels of the LORD'S house, and all that is carried away captive, from Babylon into this place.**

We might have expected **Jeremiah** immediately to denounce **Hananiah** as a false prophet (as he did in vv. 15-17). Instead, Jeremiah's initial response in verse 6 has puzzled Bible students. Jeremiah said, **Amen: the LORD do so,** or "Wonderful! I hope the LORD will do this!" (TEV).

As we try to understand this unexpected response, two related questions confront us: (1) Were Jeremiah's words spoken sarcastically or sincerely? (2) Did Jeremiah know right away that Hananiah was wrong, or did Jeremiah think that God may have given Hananiah a more recent word than he had received?

Some Bible students feel that if we had heard Jeremiah's tone of voice we would know whether he spoke sarcastically. If Jeremiah did speak sarcastically, then he knew immediately that Hananiah was wrong.

Could Jeremiah have had any doubts about who was speaking the truth—he or Hananiah? We know from other passages in the Book of Jeremiah that Jeremiah had times of confusion and doubt (see 15:10-21). Perhaps he so wanted Hananiah's words to be true that he wondered if the Lord had given Hananiah a more recent word than he had received earlier in the year. This would explain why Jeremiah confronted Hananiah confidently only after he had received reaffirmation from God (see 28:12-17).

However, even if Jeremiah knew that Hananiah was wrong, his words in verse 6 still may have been sincere. No doubt Jeremiah sincerely wished that the optimistic words of Hananiah were true. Andrew Blackwood, Jr. (*Commentary on Jeremiah*, 202) believed Jeremiah's words were more of a prayer than a wish.

Verses 7-9: Nevertheless hear thou now this word that I speak in thine ears, and in the ears of all the people; ⁸The prophets that have been before me and before thee of old prophesied both against many countries, and against great kingdoms, of war, and of evil, and of pestilence. ⁹The prophet which prophesieth of peace, when the word of the prophet shall come to pass, then shall the prophet be known, that the LORD hath truly sent him.

Jeremiah warned Hananiah, **Nevertheless hear thou now this word that I speak in thine ears, and in the ears of all the people.** Jeremiah did not claim to be speaking for the Lord, but he was speaking the truth as he saw it. He made two points.

First, Jeremiah reminded Hananiah that **the prophets . . . of old,** those who came **before** their time, usually had **prophesied both against many countries, and against great kingdoms, of war, and of evil, and of pestilence.** In other words, they were prophets of judgment who spoke unpopular messages that did not please the people of their times.

Second, Jeremiah said that the burden of proof was on the exception to the rule—that is, on **the prophet which prophesieth of peace.** The only way for such a crowd-pleasing prophet's message to be proven to be true is if what he predicted comes true: **When the word of the prophet shall come to pass, then shall the prophet be known, that the LORD hath truly sent him.** As an old proverb says, "The proof of the pudding is in the eating" (Bergen Evans, ed., *Dictionary of Quotations* [New York: Avenel Books, 1978], 559). Of course, only in retrospect can we judge a prophet on this basis.

Because a message is pleasing does not ensure that it is true. Believers are to realize that sometimes only time will tell whether a message proved to be true.

3. Confident or Credible? (Jer. 28:10-13)

Enough talk; now it was time for action.

Verses 10-11: **Then Hananiah the prophet took the yoke from off the prophet Jeremiah's neck, and brake it. ¹¹And Hananiah spake in the presence of all the people, saying, Thus saith the Lord; Even so will I break the yoke of Nebuchadnezzar king of Babylon from the neck of all nations within the space of two full years. And the prophet Jeremiah went his way.**

Hananiah was emboldened by Jeremiah's failure to confront and denounce him right away. Jeremiah often used acts to symbolize his messages. The **yoke** of wood Jeremiah wore was an example of prophetic symbolism. Every time the people saw Jeremiah and his yoke, they were reminded of God's word about Nebuchadnezzar's coming victory over Judah (chap. 27). Now Hananiah used this for an act of prophetic symbolism of his own. He **took the yoke from off the prophet Jeremiah's neck, and brake it.** Then Hananiah declared that this action meant that God would **break the yoke of Nebuchadnezzar king of Babylon from the neck of all nations.** Hananiah repeated his earlier prediction that God would do this **within the space of two full years.**

Jeremiah's response to this confident prediction has puzzled Bible students as much as his response in verse 6. **The prophet Jeremiah** simply **went his way** without any further verbal response. Some interpreters believe that Jeremiah was trusting God to vindicate him and to show Hananiah to be a liar. In other words, verses 10-11 set forth the test of truth based on whether a prophet's words come true. God would show Hananiah to be a false prophet by events of the next two years. When Nebuchadnezzar's yoke remained, people would know Hananiah was a false prophet.

Another possibility is that Jeremiah did not reply immediately because he was waiting for God to tell him how to respond to this announcement by Hananiah. Jeremiah probably still believed that his original prophecy in chapter 27 was from God and that God had not changed His mind, but he waited for the Lord to confirm this.

True and false prophets cannot be distinguished by how confident they sound. Often false prophets sound even more confident than true prophets. We speak of "con" men. Remember that *con* is short for *confidence*. These people are experts at gaining the confidence of their intended victims. If a lie is told often enough and with enough confidence, many people will believe it—especially if voices of truth have been silenced.

Verses 12-13: Then the word of the LORD came unto Jeremiah the prophet, after that Hananiah the prophet had broken the yoke from off the neck of the prophet Jeremiah, saying, ¹³Go and tell Hananiah, saying, Thus saith the LORD; Thou hast broken the yokes of wood; but thou shalt make for them yokes of iron.

We do not know how much time passed between the event in verse 11 and that in verse 12. **Then** could have been almost right away or it could have been longer. But eventually, **the word of the LORD came unto Jeremiah the prophet.** This true prophet of God was to deliver God's message to Hananiah. In essence, God repeated the message of chapter 27. The difference was that whereas Hananiah had **broken the yokes of wood,** God now promised **yokes of iron** would be put on the people. **Wood** might be broken, but not **iron.** In other words, God reaffirmed and strengthened His earlier word.

4. Persuasive or Authentic? (Jer. 28:15-17)

Jeremiah had remained silent for a while; but when he clearly heard God's word, he spoke boldly and confidently. He might have been the only one speaking the message, but if he was sure it was God's word, he was ready to speak it, no matter what the cost.

Martin Luther was a kind of 16th-century Jeremiah. Based on his study of the Scriptures, he had come to experience what Paul called being justified by faith. This doctrine was diametrically opposed to the official position of the established church of his day. Luther boldly wrote and preached God's truth. Inevitably Luther was called before the powerful political and religious leaders of the day. He was ordered to deny the truth of what he had written or to face the consequences.

The official written record of Luther's response was this: "Unless I am convicted by Scripture or plain reason—I do not accept the authority of popes and councils, for they have contradicted each other—my conscience is captive to the Word of God. I cannot and I will not recant anything, for to go against conscience is neither right nor safe. God help me. Amen."

Roland H. Bainton, a church historian and biographer of Luther, noted that the earliest printed version added the words: "Here I stand, I cannot do otherwise" (Roland H. Bainton, *Here I Stand* [New York: A Mentor Book, 1958], 144). Such was the stand Jeremiah took.

Verses 15-17: **Then said the prophet Jeremiah unto Hananiah the prophet, Hear now, Hananiah; The LORD hath not sent thee; but thou makest this people to trust in a lie. ¹⁶Therefore thus saith the LORD; Behold, I will cast thee from off the face of the earth: this year thou shalt die, because thou hast taught rebellion against the LORD. ¹⁷So Hananiah the prophet died the same year in the seventh month.**

Through Jeremiah, the Lord accused Hananiah of three serious sins: (1) Although **the LORD** had **not sent** him, Hananiah had claimed to be coming from the Lord and bearing the Lord's word. (2) As a result, Hananiah led the **people to trust in a lie.** (3) Hananiah thus **taught rebellion against the LORD.**

The Bible clearly warns false prophets about all these sins. Those who claim to be **sent** by the Lord truly must have been sent by Him. Otherwise, such liars and deceivers will face death (Deut. 18:20). By causing people to **trust in a lie,** false prophets cause people to place their confidence in something that is totally unworthy of people's trust. Such misplaced trusts spell disaster for those who believe the lies and for those who tell the lies (Jer. 23:16-40).

Hananiah might have objected to the accusation of inciting people to rebel against the Lord, but his message included resisting Nebuchadnezzar, whom the Lord had announced as His instrument of judgment on Judah. Through Jeremiah, the Lord had commanded the people to submit to Nebuchadnezzar, God's chosen vessel of judgment. By resisting Nebuchadnezzar, they were rebelling **against the LORD.** Hananiah and other false prophets thus were inciting **rebellion against the LORD.** According to the law, this was not only a sin but a crime deserving death (Deut. 13:5; 18:20). Therefore God pronounced a judgment of death on Hananiah. **I will cast thee from off the face of the earth** meant that Hananiah would die that year. The fulfillment of this prophet word is recorded in verse 17: **So Hananiah the prophet died the same year in the seventh month.**

As believers, we need to be aware that God will judge deceptive messengers who persuade people to rebel against the Lord; people who believe the messengers' lies are also in danger of judgment. William Cullen Bryant said it well:

> Truth, crushed to earth, shall rise again;
> Th' eternal years of God are hers;
> But Error, wounded, writhes in pain,
> And dies among his worshippers.

("The Battlefield," *American Quotations,* ed. by Gorton Carruth and Eugene Ehrlich [New York: Wings Books, 1994], 558.)

Four questions should help every believer distinguish true from false messengers:

1. Is the messenger more concerned with popularity than with truth?

2. Is the messenger's goal to speak words that please the right people or to speak God's Word—no matter how displeasing the message may be to the hearers?

3. Is the messenger's confidence based on human factors or on the Word of God?

4. How well does the message stand the test of time?

August 23

TRUE OR FALSE HOPE?

Background Scripture: Jeremiah 29:1-32
Focal Verses: Jeremiah 29:1-2,4-14

INTRODUCTION

1. People sometimes wonder, *What hope do I have in times of turmoil?*
2. Our English word *hope* often means little more than wishful thinking. Such hope does not provide any sound basis for real security. Ultimately, such hope proves deceitful and leads to despair. By contrast, biblical hope is more than wishful thinking because it is based on God and His sure promises.
3. The Lesson Bible Truth is that God's good purposes for His people give them hope in times of turmoil.
4. The Lesson Outcome is to help you find true hope in God and His purposes for your life.

I. SOME PRELIMINARY CONSIDERATIONS

1. Hope and Security

Adults have experiences that add to the turmoil of turbulent times. Changes in themselves, in their families, and in society are a normal part of adult life. Many adults have failed—or feel they have failed—in various areas of their lives: marriages, parenting, careers, personal relationships, and so on. In our modern mobile society, many adults are separated from people and places that once provided a sense of security and stability. False hopes contribute to the problem by creating false expectations, which eventually lead to disappointment, despair, depression, and doubt. Confident hope in God and His promises, however, provides stability and security, even in life's darkest hours.

2. Judgment and Hope

Like many other Old Testament prophets, Jeremiah's two main themes were judgment and hope. Before the exile, most of Jeremiah's messages majored on the certainty of divine judgment. As the end neared, Jeremiah began to preach more and more messages of hope. This week's lesson features Jeremiah's letter to the early exiles in Babylon. Jeremiah refuted the false hopes of those who promised a short exile and swift destruction of the Babylonians. Instead, Jeremiah advised the exiles to settle down and to make the best of life in Babylon; however, on the basis of the word of the Lord, he promised an end of the exile within 70 years.

II.   FOCAL VERSES EXAMINED (Jer. 29:1-2,4-14)

Ancient Near Eastern society left records of many letters. In fact, Jeremiah 29 mentions four letters: one from Jeremiah to the exiles in Babylon (vv. 1-15,21-23), one from Shemaiah [shih-MAY-yuh] in Babylon to Zephaniah [zef-uh-NIGH-uh] in Jerusalem (vv. 25-28), one from Jeremiah to Shemaiah (v. 24), and a second letter to the exiles (vv. 31-32).

1. People Need Hope (Jer. 29:1-2)

People need hope. But they especially need hope when they have experienced failure, been uprooted, or lost control of areas of their lives.

Verses 1-2: Now these are the words of the letter that Jeremiah the prophet sent from Jerusalem unto the residue of the elders which were carried away captives, and to the priests, and to the prophets, and to all the people whom Nebuchadnezzar had carried away captive from Jerusalem to Babylon; ²(after that Jeconiah the king, and the queen, and the eunuchs, the princes of Judah and Jerusalem, and the carpenters, and the smiths, were departed from Jerusalem).

The opening words of verse 1 alert us to the fact that the following verses are **the words of the letter that Jeremiah the prophet sent from Jerusalem.** Jeremiah wrote to those **whom Nebuchadnezzar had carried away captive from Jerusalem to Babylon.** Verse 2 tells us that this was not the final group of exiles after the fall of Jerusalem and the destruction in 587 B.C. Instead it was an earlier group of exiles taken in 597 B.C. (compare 2 Kings 24:10-16 to Jer. 29:1-2). This exile took place as a result of a rebellion against Nebuchadnezzar by Jehoiakim [jih-HOY-uh-kim] (2 Kings 24:1). But Jehoiakim died before Nebuchadnezzar arrived to put down the rebellion (2 Kings 24:6). Jehoiakim was succeeded by his son Jehoiachin [jih-HOY-uh-kin] (2 Kings 24:6-10). **Jeconiah** [jek-oh-NIGH-uh] is another name for "Jehoiachin" (NIV).

The young king had the good sense to surrender to the overwhelming power of the Babylonians. As punishment, **Nebuchadnezzar** took back to Babylon **the king** and **the queen.** Although among the captives were "the king's wives," **the queen** in this verse probably was Nehushta [nih-HUHSH-tuh], the "queen mother" (NIV) or "king's mother" (see 2 Kings 24:8,15). **Eunuchs** probably refers to "court officials" (NIV), not to eunuchs in the physical sense. Also taken captive were **the princes of Judah and Jerusalem, and the carpenters, and the smiths. Carpenters** were general "craftsmen" (NIV), and **smiths** were "artisans" (NIV).

Verse 1 mentions among the exiles who received Jeremiah's letter **the residue of the elders. Residue** could mean "surviving" (NIV) or "the rest" (NASB). This could refer to **the elders** who survived the trip to Babylon; however, some Bible scholars think it refers to the elders who survived Nebuchadnezzar's punishment for a rebellion that took place after the exiles arrived in Babylon. In fact, ancient Babylonian records refer to a rebellion in Babylon about 595-594 B.C. in which some of the exiled Jews may have been involved.

If this is an accurate interpretation of verses 1 and 21-22, the date of Jeremiah's letter was probably in 594 B.C. If not, then at least we can say that it was written between 597 B.C., when Je-

hoiachin was taken to Babylon, and 587 B.C., when Jerusalem
was destroyed. When Jeremiah wrote, Jerusalem and the temple were still standing. We know this because false prophets
were promising the exiles that the city of Jerusalem would
never be destroyed (see vv. 8-9). Verse 1 tells us that Jeremiah
wrote not only **to the residue of the elders** but also **to the
priests, and to the prophets, and to all the people.**

When life falls in on us, we tend to lose heart and lose hope.
In every congregation, in every Sunday School class, and in
every Bible study group are people who need hope. They need
the Bible's message of confident hope based on the goodness of
God and His sure promises for the present and the future.

2. Live in Hope (Jer. 29:4-7)

Confident hope in God enables people to live peaceful, productive, and prayerful lives even in unhappy situations.

Verse 4: **Thus saith the LORD of hosts, the God of Israel, unto all that are carried away captives, whom I
have caused to be carried away from Jerusalem unto
Babylon.**

Jeremiah wrote to the captives in the name of **the LORD of
hosts, the God of Israel.** God's message was that He is Sover-
eign over all nations. The Babylonians were able to defeat
Judah only because **the LORD of hosts** used them as instruments of His wrath. **The LORD of hosts,** not Nebuchadnezzar,
carried His people into captivity. Notice the use of **I** in verses 4
and 7: **I have caused to be carried away from Jerusalem
unto Babylon** and **I have caused you to be carried away
captives.** Later, in verses 10-14, Jeremiah explained God's good
purpose in doing this.

Verses 5-6: **Build ye houses, and dwell in them; and
plant gardens, and eat the fruit of them; ⁶take ye wives,
and beget sons and daughters; and take wives for your
sons, and give your daughters to husbands, that they may
bear sons and daughters; that ye may be increased there,
and not diminished.**

The false prophets were encouraging the exiles not to unpack because God was about to send them home. Jeremiah promised that God would send the Jews back home, but only after 70 years. In the meanwhile, therefore, Jeremiah advised the exiles to settle down and make the best of their lives in Babylon. Basically, he told them to get over their grief and to go on with their lives. He named a number of practical activities that this would involve: **Build ye houses, and dwell in them; and plant gardens, and eat the fruit of them.** The normal activities of marriage and raising children were to be engaged in. The **wives,** of course, were to be Jewish maidens. In this way, the number of Jews would **be increased** while the exiles were in Babylon, **not diminished.**

Verse 7: **And seek the peace of the city whither I have caused you to be carried away captives, and pray unto the LORD for it: for in the peace thereof shall ye have peace.**

This verse contains the most striking words of **the LORD** to His exiled people. He told them **to seek the peace of the city whither I have caused you to be carried away captives.** Again God made clear that He had carried them into captivity. He also made sure that no one thought **the city** for whose **peace** they were to **pray** was Jerusalem. The Jews always have sought the peace of Jerusalem. Here, however, God commanded them to do the same thing for the capital city of their captors and enemies.

Peace translates the Hebrew word *shalom.* The word has a rich, full meaning, which our English word *peace* only partially communicates. The basic meaning of *shalom* is "well-being" and "wholeness." As used in the Bible, it refers to the well-being of each person in proper harmony with God, with other people, and with the rest of God's creation (see Robert J. Dean, *God's Big Little Words* [Nashville: Broadman Press, 1975], 106).

Thus **seek the peace of the city** meant to **pray unto the LORD for it.** This teaching foreshadows the New Testament emphasis on loving our enemies, which includes praying for them and doing good for them (see Matt. 5:43-48 and Rom. 12:17-21). More often than not, the Hebrews called on God to punish their enemies; but the Lord told the exiles to pray for Babylon.

The result of such actions would benefit not only the Babylonian captors but also the Jewish exiles. God promised, **in the peace thereof shall ye have peace.** Insofar as peace reigned in Babylon, the peace of the exiles would be increased. Paul told the early Christians to pray for their Roman rulers for the same reason: "I urge, then, first of all, that requests, prayers, intercession and thanksgiving be made for everyone—for kings and all those in authority, that we may live peaceful and quiet lives in all godliness and holiness" (1 Tim. 2:1-2, NIV).

Before Jeremiah told the exiles the reason for hope (vv. 10-14), he told them how to act. His advice was to go on with life in as normal a way as possible, and above all, to act in love toward others. This is good advice for anyone who is discouraged, depressed, or in despair. No matter how you may feel, do what you know God wants you to do. With God's help, He can move you beyond some of your negative feelings; but don't wait until your feelings are bright and positive to do what is right and good.

3. Beware of False Hope (Jer. 29:8-9)

When people need real hope, raising false hope results in further turmoil and eventually in disillusionment.

Verses 8-9: **For thus saith the LORD of hosts, the God of Israel; Let not your prophets and your diviners, that be in the midst of you, deceive you, neither hearken to your dreams which ye cause to be dreamed. [9]For they prophesy falsely unto you in my name: I have not sent them, saith the LORD.**

Verses 8-9 help explain why **the LORD of hosts, the God of Israel** sent these words to the exiles in a letter from Jeremiah. There were **prophets** and **diviners** who were **in the midst of** the exiles in Babylon, just as there were back in Judah. Like the false prophets in Judah, the ones in Babylon had not been sent by God. God warned the exiles not to let their prophets and diviners **deceive** them. They deceived the people by prophesying **falsely,** that is, by prophesying "lies" (NIV). Some of the false prophets based their predictions on **dreams.** Apparently some of the exiles were encouraging these dreamers because the Lord said, **Neither hearken to your dreams which ye cause to be dreamed,** or better, "Do not listen to the dreams you encourage them to have" (NIV). The deceived people continued to hope that Jerusalem and the temple would never be destroyed.

The Greeks had a myth about Pandora's box. The box was filled with evils. Pandora was told not to open the box, but curiosity led her to peek into it. When she did, all kinds of evils were let loose to plague humanity. She quickly closed the box, but all that was left was hope. The Greeks had mixed feelings about whether hope was a blessing or a curse. Many considered hope to be the worst of evils because it lures people on with deceptive promises of better times, but in the end hope leads to disaster and finally to death.

If the only hope we have is based on human resources, then hope is dangerous. The false prophets in Babylon were feeding the hopes of the exiles for a quick solution to their problems. This kept them from doing what Jeremiah told them to do—settle down for a long exile. When the people's hopes proved false, they would be plunged into deeper despair. Beware of placing your hope in anything or anyone other than God and His Word.

4. Trust in God's Good Purposes (Jer. 29:10-14)

God's long-range promises to His people provide a basis for confident hope for the future and for security in the present.

Verses 10-11: **For thus saith the LORD, That after seventy years be accomplished at Babylon I will visit you, and perform my good word toward you, in causing you to return to this place. ¹¹For I know the thoughts that I think toward you, saith the LORD, thoughts of peace, and not of evil, to give you an expected end.**

In an earlier sermon in 605 B.C., Jeremiah accused the people of Judah of persistently refusing to listen to the long line of prophets whom the Lord had sent to them (25:1-7). As a result, Judah and Jerusalem would be laid waste by the hand of the Lord's servant Nebuchadnezzar (vv. 8-10). After the Jews served the Babylonians for 70 years, the Babylonians would be punished by God (vv. 11-14). In the letter to the exiles, Jeremiah made the same points in the reverse order. Jeremiah again predicted 70 years for the Babylonians and for the captivity of the Jews (29:10-14). Jeremiah also again predicted the fall of Jerusalem (vv. 15-18) because they had refused to hear God's prophets (v. 19).

These passages mention **seventy years** for Babylon and for Judah's exile. **Be accomplished at Babylon** seems to refer to the end of the Babylonian Empire's hold over the Jews. After **seventy years,** God promised to **return** the Jews **to this place,** that is, to Jerusalem. Bible students debate whether the **seventy years** was intended to refer to an exact number of years or was a round number, possibly representing about the life span of a human being (Ps. 90:10). Everyone agrees that Jeremiah's prediction struck a blow at the false prophets, who were predicting a quick victory over Babylon and an almost immediate return to Jerusalem. Jeremiah held out hope for a return, but not within the lifetime of most of the adult exiles.

God, who earlier had claimed that He was the One who carried Judah into captivity (vv. 4,7), now said that He was the One who would **visit** them and cause them to **return to** Judah. Although He intended to punish His people, God's long-range purpose for them was for **peace, and not . . . evil.** He would **perform** His **good word,** or "gracious purpose" (NIV), **toward** them. As a result, God was giving them **an expected end,** or better, "hope and a future" (NIV) or "a future filled with hope" (CEV).

Verses 12-14: **Then shall ye call upon me, and ye shall go and pray unto me, and I will hearken unto you.** [13]**And ye shall seek me, and find me, when ye shall search for me with all your heart.** [14]**And I will be found of you, saith the LORD: and I will turn away your captivity, and I will gather you from all the nations, and from all the places whither I have driven you, saith the LORD; and I will bring you again into the place whence I caused you to be carried away captive.**

This return would be accompanied by a change of heart by the Jews. Notice what Jeremiah said that the Jews would do toward God: **Call upon me . . . go and pray unto me . . . seek me . . . find me . . . search for me with all your heart.**

God in turn would **hearken unto** them. Note all the ways God described what He would do for His people: **I will be found of you . . . I will turn away your captivity . . . I will gather you from all the nations . . . I will bring you again into the place whence I caused you to be carried away captive** (v. 14).

Jeremiah foretold a bright future for God's people. And the basis for this confident hope was the sure **word** of God, whose nature, plans, and promises are **good** (v. 10).

Some people who profess to believe in the God of the Bible experience so many troubles that they conclude that God does not care or that He can do nothing to help them. They doubt the goodness of God—and sometimes even accuse God of evil.

Christians dare to believe that God is good. His purposes and gifts are good, not evil (Jas. 1:13-17). In the worse of life's evil experiences, God is at work to bring good out of the evil (Rom. 8:28; 2 Cor. 12:7-9). In "The Eternal Goodness," John Greenleaf Whittier (1807–1892) expressed this basic faith. Here is one of the many powerful affirmations in his testimony:

> Yet, in the maddening maze of things,
>   And tossed by storm and flood,
> To one fixed trust my spirit clings;
>   I know that God is good!

(*Masterpieces of Religious Verse,* ed. by James Dalton Morrison [New York: Harper and Row, Publishers, 1948], 69-70.)

Trust in the goodness of God is the basis for the kind of confident hope that enables believers to endure life's worst experiences. In the crucifixion and resurrection of Jesus Christ, God not only opened the way to salvation and eternal life, but He also showed us that He suffers with us and for us—we are never alone in life's worst times—and that He has the final word over suffering, pain, sorrow, sin, and death. None of these things can separate us from Him and His love. So have hope. Have hope even in times of turmoil. But let your hope be in God.

August 30

LIVING BY FAITH OR BY SIGHT?

Background Scripture: Jeremiah 31:31-34; 32:1-44
Focal Verses: Jeremiah 31:33-34; 32:1-3,6-7,8b-9.
13-15,21-22

INTRODUCTION

1. This is the fifth and final lesson in the unit on "Finding Security in a Turbulent World." This lesson reinforces the basic lesson on finding in God our only real and lasting source of security.

2. But you may have asked yourself, *Why should I take God at His word when I can't see that He's doing anything?*

3. Many adults base their values and decisions on things they can see and count. However, none of these things is secure permanently. People of faith base their ultimate trust in the yet unfulfilled promises of the invisible God. Believing adults base such faith on the faithfulness of God in keeping past promises.

4. The Lesson Bible Truth is that God's faithfulness in keeping His promises strengthens believers' sense of security in turbulent times.

5. The Lesson Outcome is to help you trust God to keep His promises even when you can't see that He's doing anything.

6. This lesson is the evangelism lesson for this quarter.

I. SOME PRELIMINARY CONSIDERATIONS

1. Believing Is Seeing

People often quote the saying, "Seeing is believing." They mean by this that they will believe only in things that can be proven to them by natural means. The words and actions of people show whether they live by faith or by sight. Hebrews 11:1 describes faith as "the substance of things hoped for, the evidence of things not seen." The people of faith in Hebrews 11 and else-

where in the Bible had discovered that life's greatest realities—
God and His kingdom—are seen only by faith. In other words,
"Believing is seeing." Finding security in God involves living by
faith in an unseen God and His as yet unfulfilled promises.

2. Hope in the Darkest Times

Jeremiah was in prison. Jerusalem was undergoing its final
siege. The nation of Judah was about to be destroyed. Many of
the Jewish people would be killed or deported to Babylon. But as
the end for Jerusalem and Judah neared and came, Jeremiah increasingly turned from messages of doom to messages of hope.
Jeremiah 30–33 is called the Book of Consolation or the Book of
Comfort because these chapters contain messages of comfort and
hope. And what Jeremiah did at this time showed his faith in
God's promise to restore the nation to the land after the Babylonian captivity. It was just the right moment for a heroic example
of faith, an action based on hope, in spite of the turbulent times.

II. FOCAL VERSES EXAMINED
(Jer. 31:33-34; 32:1-3,6-7,8b-9,13-15,21-22)

Jeremiah 32 records a prophecy of faith and hope that God
commanded Jeremiah to proclaim by a dramatic symbolic act as
well as by his words. God told Jeremiah to purchase his cousin's
field as a sign of His promise that Judah would be restored in
the future. Chapter 32 thus falls into two main parts: the purchase of the field (vv. 1-15) and a dialog between Jeremiah and
the Lord (vv. 16-44). Jeremiah 31:31-34 is a high point in the
Old Testament as Jeremiah looked into the future and prophesied concerning God's new covenant. Obviously, this passage
held tremendous impact for New Testament doctrine.

1. Visible Sources of Security Will Fail (Jer. 32:1-3)

Chapter 32 begins the second half of Jeremiah's Book of Consolation. This portion is entirely in prose.

Verses 1-3: **The word that came to Jeremiah from the LORD in the tenth year of Zedekiah king of Judah, which was the eighteenth year of Nebuchadrezzar. ²For then the king of Babylon's army besieged Jerusalem: and Jeremiah the prophet was shut up in the court of the prison, which was in the king of Judah's house. ³For Zedekiah king of Judah had shut him up, saying, Wherefore dost thou prophesy, and say, Thus saith the LORD, Behold, I will give this city into the hand of the king of Babylon, and he shall take it.**

Four facts mentioned in verses 1-2 help us date this **word** of prophesy that came to Jeremiah. First, it came during the **tenth year of Zedekiah king of Judah.** Second, it came during the **eighteenth year of Nebuchadrezzar . . . king of Babylon.** Third, it happened when **the king of Babylon's army besieged Jerusalem.** Fourth, it was when **Jeremiah the prophet was shut up in the court of the prison.** Thus the date was 588/587 B.C. **Nebuchadrezzar** [neb-yoo-kad-DREZ-uhr] is a variation of the spelling for "Nebuchadnezzar" [neb-yoo-kad-NEZ-uhr] (NIV).

Jeremiah 37 sheds further light on the events of the siege of Jerusalem. At the beginning of the siege, Jeremiah was free to come and go. During the Babylonian siege of Jerusalem, Pharaoh's army marched toward Jerusalem. The Babylonians temporarily lifted their siege of Jerusalem as they prepared to meet the oncoming Egyptians. During this time, Jeremiah tried to visit his home area; however, he was arrested and accused of deserting to the Babylonians. Jeremiah denied the charge, but he was punished by being thrown into the dungeon. Later, the king of Judah had him moved to **the court of the prison.** Meanwhile, the Egyptians retreated and the Babylonians resumed their siege of Jerusalem. Jerusalem fell in the 11th year of King Zedekiah [zed-uh-KIGH-uh], which was 587 B.C. (Jer. 39:2).

During most of Jeremiah's ministry, he had preached messages that were unpopular with the leaders and people of Judah. He had condemned sin and predicted judgment. As time passed, he became increasingly specific about the form this judgment would take. Jeremiah predicted that Nebuchadrezzar and the Babylonians would conquer Judah and destroy

Jerusalem and the temple. This was not only an unpopular message; the king and people considered Jeremiah a traitor. When **Zedekiah king of Judah** asked, **Wherefore dost thou prophesy,** he was asking Jeremiah, "Why do you prophesy as you do?" (NIV). Jeremiah had prophesied based on what **the LORD** had said. Thus the answer to the king's question was that it was **the word ... from the LORD** and, however unpopular it was or treasonous it sounded, it was the truth.

All the people of Judah's sources of security were based on what they could see: the temple, their army, the walls of Jerusalem. Jeremiah warned the king and the people that all their sources of security would fail. And so it is today. All who trust in visible sources of security are building on something that ultimately will fail; only God and His kingdom are secure.

2. Faith Sees Beyond the Apparent
(Jer. 32:6-7,8b-9,13-15)

Verse 6 resumes the introduction from verse 1 (vv. 2-5 are parenthetical). The Lord's words of instruction to Jeremiah are in verse 7. The fulfillment of the Lord's words began immediately.

Verses 6-7,8b-9: **And Jeremiah said, The word of the LORD came unto me, saying, [7]Behold, Hanameel the son of Shallum thine uncle shall come unto thee, saying, Buy thee my field that is in Anathoth: for the right of redemption is thine to buy it.... [8b]Then I knew that this was the word of the LORD. [9]And I bought the field of Hanameel my uncle's son, that was in Anathoth, and weighed him the money, even seventeen shekels of silver.**

The word of the LORD came to Jeremiah, telling him that his cousin **Hanameel** [huh-NAM-ih-el] (an alternate spelling for the NIV's "Hanamel" [HAN-uh-mehl]) was coming to see him. Hanameel was coming to ask Jeremiah to **buy** his **field** in **Anathoth** [AN-uh-thawth], Jeremiah's hometown (1:1). This offer to sell was based on **the right of redemption,** an Old Testament law about keeping land within a family. This was achieved by a relative, called a kinsman-redeemer, buying the land (see Lev. 25:25-34; Ruth 4:1-10). When Hanameel made this request of Jeremiah, the prophet **knew** that what he heard was **the word of the LORD.** Therefore, Jeremiah bought the field for **seventeen shekels of silver.**

Verses 13-15: **And I charged Baruch before them, saying, ¹⁴Thus saith the LORD of hosts, the God of Israel; Take these evidences, this evidence of the purchase, both which is sealed, and this evidence which is open; and put them in an earthen vessel, that they may continue many days. ¹⁵For thus saith the LORD of hosts, the God of Israel; Houses and fields and vineyards shall be possessed again in this land.**

The prophet was careful to purchase the land legally and in such a way that everyone knew about it. Because Jeremiah was confined, he asked **Baruch** [BAY-rook]—the one who wrote down the words that the prophet dictated (36:4,18)—to handle the details of the sale. In the presence of official witnesses Jeremiah **charged** Baruch, "Take these documents, both the sealed and unsealed copies of the deed of purchase, and put them in a clay jar so they will last a long time" (NIV). This was an act of prophetic symbolism. The spoken message, of which the deeds of purchase were the symbols, is in verse 15: **The LORD of hosts, the God of Israel** promised, **Houses and fields and vineyards shall be possessed again in this land.** This prophecy was consistent with Jeremiah's earlier promises that the Lord would restore the people of Judah to their land after 70 years (25:11-12; 29:10).

Consider how shocked the people must have been when Jeremiah bought this land. He adamantly was predicting defeat by the Babylonians. He announced that the Babylonians would leave the city and land in ruins and that the survivors would go into exile. Why then would Jeremiah buy land when he himself said that the nation was about to fall?

Jeremiah bought the field because the Lord commanded him to do it in order to deliver the message of hope in verse 15. Jeremiah knew that neither he nor scarcely any of the other adults would live to see it, but the Lord was going to bring the Jews back to Judah. Jeremiah thus never expected personally to live on the land or to benefit from it in any material way. After the

Babylonians came, the land would be virtually worthless. However, God had a long-range plan of hope for His people. Jeremiah walked by faith, not by sight. His God was unseen to human eyes, and His promise of restoration was unfulfilled; yet Jeremiah dared to believe that God was real and His promises were sure. We, like Jeremiah, must learn that faith sees beyond what is apparent, and we must learn to trust God to fulfill His promises.

3. God Has Kept His Past Promises (Jer. 32:21-22)

Jeremiah 32:17-25 records Jeremiah's prayer after he had given the deeds to Baruch. Most of the prayer exalts God for His greatness, including His acts on behalf of His people (vv. 17-23). The prayer closes with an expression of wonder at what the Lord had told Jeremiah to do (vv. 24-25).

Verses 21-22: **And hast brought forth thy people Israel out of the land of Egypt with signs, and with wonders, and with a strong hand, and with a stretched out arm, and with great terror;** [22]**and hast given them this land, which thou didst swear to their fathers to give them, a land flowing with milk and honey.**

Jeremiah recalled two examples of how God had kept past promises. Jeremiah first praised the Lord for bringing **forth** His **people Israel out of the land of Egypt.** As Bible students will recall from their study of the 10 plagues, this deliverance from Egypt was done **with signs, and with wonders, and with a strong hand, and with a stretched out arm, and with great terror.** Second, Jeremiah praised the Lord for giving Israel **this land, which thou didst swear to their fathers to give them.**

Therefore, as Jeremiah placed his faith in the promises of God, he was not exercising blind gullibility with no basis in past events. Jeremiah remembered what the unseen God had done in keeping His past promises that He made to His people.

Thus another reason we believe that the invisible God will keep His as-of-yet unfulfilled promises is because of God's faithfulness in keeping His past promises. As the hymn writer wrote:

O God, our help in ages past,
Our hope for years to come,
Be Thou our guard while life shall last,
And our eternal home.

(Isaac Watts, "O God, Our Help in Ages Past," No. 74, *The Baptist Hymnal,* 1991.)

4. God's Promises Are Not Limited to the Present (Jer. 31:33-34)

Jeremiah 32 involves a symbolic act and a message of hope that came during the final days of Jerusalem. More significant is the word of the Lord that came in Jeremiah 31:31-34. This prediction of the new covenant is one of the most important passages in the Book of Jeremiah and probably the best known. This is the only reference to the new covenant in the Old Testament.

Verses 33-34: **But this shall be the covenant that I will make with the house of Israel; After those days, saith the LORD, I will put my law in their inward parts, and write it in their hearts; and will be their God, and they shall be my people. ³⁴And they shall teach no more every man his neighbor, and every man his brother, saying, Know the LORD: for thcy shall all know me, from the least of them unto the greatest of them, saith the LORD: for I will forgive their iniquity, and I will remember their sin no more.**

God led Jeremiah to describe a new **covenant,** different in some significant ways from the old covenant given at Mount Sinai. Verses 33-34 highlight three of the main distinctives of the new covenant: (1) God's law would be written internally, not externally; (2) all people of faith would have personal knowledge of God; and (3) divine forgiveness would be the foundation for the new covenant.

Under the old covenant, the Ten Commandments were written on tablets of stone; in the new covenant, God promised, **I will put my law in their inward parts, and write it in their hearts.** Under the new covenant, the external letter of the law is replaced by the inner spirit of the law, which God's Spirit writes on the minds and hearts of believers (see 2 Cor. 3:6).

The first part of verse 34 describes the old covenant's system of mediators, who told people to **know the LORD.** A characteristic of the old covenant was that it was mediated to the people by the priests and other mediators. Under the new covenant, every believer has full access to the Father through Jesus Christ, our great High Priest (see Heb. 4:14-16). This is the meaning of the words **for they shall all know me, from the least of them unto the greatest of them.**

The foundation for the new covenant is God's promise, **I will forgive their iniquity, and I will remember their sin no more.** The old covenant had at its heart the demand for obedience to the law, which the people persistently failed to do. Thus a covenant was needed that was based on God's grace, not on human obedience. This is true of the new covenant (Eph. 2:8-9).

As Christians, we live under these provisions of the new covenant (Luke 22:20; Heb. 8:7-13). However, the consummation of these promises lies in the future. We, like the people of the old covenant, still "walk by faith, not by sight" (2 Cor. 5:7). Like the Old Testament believers, Christians also are pilgrims of faith (Heb. 11:13-16,40). As people of faith, we need to realize that God's promises are not limited to the present. Thus some of His promises will be fulfilled after our lifetimes. Nevertheless, we are to take God at His word and continue to live by faith, even when we can't see that God is doing anything.

> Have faith in God tho' all else fail about you;
> Have faith in God, He provides for His own;
> He cannot fail tho' all kingdoms shall perish,
> He rules, He reigns upon His throne.

> Have faith in God, He's on His throne;
> Have faith in God, He watches o'er His own;
> He cannot fail, He must prevail;
> Have faith in God, have faith in God.

(B. B. McKinney, "Have Faith in God," No. 405, *The Baptist Hymnal,* 1991.)